The Power of Sour

The acidic nature of vinegar gives it a special ability to open our senses and make our taste buds more receptive to all the other tastes. At the same time, it also works to bring balance, toning down the intensity of overtly bitter and fatty foods. *House of Vinegar* will help you unleash this flavor booster in your own cooking with recipes for base vinegars like Begonia Vinegar, Apple Wine Vinegar, and Craft Beer Vinegar, then use these recipes as building blocks to give new life to dishes like Pickled Green Tomatoes, Spicy Peach Confit Chicken Wings, Sunday Gravy over Cavatelli, and Classic English Pea & Onion Salad. With engaging writing and gorgeous photography, *House of Vinegar* will revolutionize the way you think about flavor and change the way you cook.

HOUSE OF VINEGAR

HOUSE OF Vinegar

The Power of Sour

with Recipes

Jonathon Sawyer

photographs by **PETER LARSON** | *illustrations by* **M. SWEENEY**

TEN SPEED PRESS

California | New York

Foreword by
MICHAEL SYMON

Jon Sawyer has always walked to his own beat, and often has taken the more difficult path to get to where he is in life. He does things his way regardless of how hard it may be, and he doesn't worry about what others may think. To some, this may be most obvious when it comes to his style, but to me it is most evident in the food he cooks! In *House of Vinegar*, he really gives an inside look into what makes him tick and how he thinks about food. The best part of this is that you get to see and learn the brilliance, while he did all the research and hard work that allows you to re-create this magic easily.

Fermentation is such a trendy buzz word in kitchens these days but it is something Jon has been doing and researching throughout his entire career; learning how to intensify flavors and alter textures of food with age-old techniques and new, innovative thought

processes that create exciting flavors that are all his own. From the minute I met him when he was a young cook, I knew there was something very special about him. His passion and eagerness to not only continue to learn but to also push the envelope and experiment with foods is unmatched in this industry. It made being around him always so inspiring. Watching him find himself as a chef and then continue to gain the confidence and trust in not only himself but of those around him has been one of my great joys as a chef.

What makes Jon Sawyer a great man, husband, father, and chef is his ability to block out the outside noise. As I sit and read this book, I find that he has inspired me once again and, as always, is making me hungry and excited to get into the kitchen and start cooking and to let everyone know what Jon has known all along there is definitely power in the sour!

INTRODUCTION: NOTES FROM A Vinegar-Loving Superfan

I decided to become a vinegar-maker when I was in a brightly lit home-goods department store in downtown Manhattan. It was the early 2000s, and I was an overworked and underpaid chef who found myself with a night off.

I wanted to cook dinner for my girl (who's now [Borat voice] my wife, Amelia), but when I went through the pantry of our Lower East Side apartment, I found dust bunnies—no vinegar. I already needed to go out to pick up the chicken I had planned to cook, so I asked Amelia if she wanted to go with me to grab some vinegar. Our dinner was in dire need of a dank, baller bottle. The restaurant I cooked in at the time, Kitchen 22, stood strongly behind a three-vinegar pantry: crappy red wine vinegar for sauce work, rice vinegar for pickles, and sherry vinegar for vinaigrettes. We also rocked the balsamic drizzle that was ubiquitous in the 1990s. (I still hate balsamic vinegar with bread to this day, and I solely blame it on this stupid craze.)

Anyway, none of these was what I was going for that night. I wanted to splurge, and I wanted something interesting. At the store,

an oddly happy clerk led us over to the "fancy vinegar" section. I perused the shelves and settled on a stunning ceramic cask of California Cabernet vinegar. Twenty-nine dollars later (a hefty sum for a broke-ass cook paying $1,650 per month for rent), we left the store, armed with my secret weapon. I couldn't have been happier; I had some potent vinegar in one hand and my girlfriend's hand in the other. We trekked back to our tiny apartment on Rivington Street, ready for a romantic night in.

As I prepared my mise en place, I noticed the vinegar was unusually dark in color. I opened the bottle and was not superhappy with how it tasted, so I thought, crap, I had not taken the time to read the label. When I did, I found that there was caramel coloring in it, and it was one of the main ingredients. "Why caramel coloring?" I ranted aloud. Amelia listened to me preach, as I'm wont to do, about vinegar in America. For that precious expenditure, I could have had a *great* bottle of California Cabernet vinegar, or a classic European vinegar. However, I couldn't find an American regionally sourced vinegar made with simple ingredients.

I continued to vent, but Amelia, tired of my tirade and hungry as hell, said, "Why don't you fucking make it then?" And like Alice down the rabbit hole, my path as a chef took a twisted turn. For the following decade I made sure my familiarity with sour vernacular evolved from beginner's terms like *sherry*, *distilled*, and *red wine* to *SCOBY*, *mother*, *fermentation*, and *Acetobacter*. In that moment I became a vinegar-maker. And I haven't looked back since.

After that night in our tiny New York City apartment, eating our bland caramel-colored-vinegar salad, I immersed myself in all things sour. Armed with a pen and paper, I went to the New York City Public Library (which is still one of my favorite places in the world). You have to realize that at this point, the Internet was still in its early days (before fantasy football, podcasts, and porn were only a few finger taps away on your smartphone), so I focused on books and papers to learn the process of making vinegar. I tapped into the engineering education I gained while attending the University of Dayton (shout out to the Flyers for the knowledge and the debt) to sketch my next

steps. I came up with prototypes for my varieties of specific vinegars and utilized Sandor Katz's *Wild Fermentation*, which came out during these initial vinegar-making years, as my compass.

The first batches of vinegar that I made were Chardonnay from Burgundy, a Cabernet from California, and, for my Welsh-Italian wife (a fan of fish and chips), a malted style of beer vinegar. My pantry, formerly home to dust bunnies and a certain ceramic cask, overflowed with my experiments. Within months, I had a pretty stunning beer vinegar on my hands. The wine vinegars were soon to follow. Having quick success with my first experiments definitely encouraged the rapid growth of our vinegar company.

My cooking career has taken me to every corner of the East Coast—and the world. I decided I wanted to be a chef while attending the University of Dayton; discovered how I wanted to cook while living in Rome, inspired by the Italians' adherence to classic technique, methodical sourcing, and balanced flavors; sharpened my skills in Pittsburgh at the Pennsylvania Institute of Culinary Arts; cut my teeth at the Biltmore Hotel in Miami; and made my first bones as a chef in NYC at Charlie Palmer's Kitchen 22 and fellow Clevelander Michael Symon's Parea.

Eventually, I found myself back in my hometown of Cleveland with my own restaurant, which provided the perfect opportunity to start the massive vinegar-making operation I'd dreamed of since those halcyon Big Apple days. At my first Cleveland spot, Bar Cento, I'd take the leftover beers from our two hundred feet of draft lines—everything from pilsners and lagers to IPAs and stouts—and place them in barrels to make something new out of them. You have to realize that

many beer-hall owners throw out hundreds of gallons of old brews every week, so I figured there was a golden opportunity to recycle these precious hops.

Company-wise, I created a set of ethics for our product: We'd never add sugar or coloring; we'd dilute only if we had an alcohol percentage that was too intense to turn the *Acetobacter* into vinegar; and we weren't going to use any industrial short-cuts like forcing oxygen into our vinegars or buying mothers (if you're not following this jargon now, stick with us—we'll explain them shortly). Our company mission is to make varietal-specific, single-origin, wild-fermented vinegars. What does this mean? Our vinegars are alive—think about the difference between kombucha and soda.

When we opened Greenhouse Tavern, these beliefs led us to exponentially increase our production. What started as a few containers in the restaurant blew up into several hundred gallons of fermenting liquid in my house's basement. Our obsession to continually churn out top-shelf sour made our neighbors believe we were whipping up meth, as we dragged more gallon barrels downstairs.

Since those early days of making vinegar, my love for it has grown greater with each new venture I've tackled. My other restaurants, Trentina (a northern Italian–inspired restaurant) and Noodlecat (a ramen joint), embrace the use of vinegar with the same passion and fervor that catapulted the Tavern into a James Beard Award win.

Even though we were doing this bootstrap-style, all of my goals at that point had been accomplished. First, we made great, regionally sourced vinegar for less than twenty dollars per bottle. Second, we made enough of that vinegar to feature it on our menus. Third, we made enough vinegar so that our restaurant wouldn't have to purchase any outside bottles for any of its recipes. Fourth, we could replace citrus-based ingredients whenever we wanted. (Spoiler: Vinegar is a great substitute for citrus.) And last, we produced enough to sell to the sour-starved public. We were self-sufficient in a way that no restaurant could claim.

That last point is something that farm-to-table restaurants (whatever that term means nowadays) take for granted. Sure, they can get meat cuts or vegetables from the local farm, but think about the little things that bring out your food's flavor—like vinegar. We truly became a northeastern Ohio restaurant in every way. It was an experiment that was not only profitable and practical but proved that anyone could produce the building blocks of flavor with an old bottle of booze and some pantry space.

Which brings me to this cookbook. Vinegar is so easy to make that it nearly happens without doing any work at all. It's so easy, in fact, that, for thousands of years, wine-makers have been trying to develop ways to prevent wine from automatically fermenting into vinegar. Don't think of this text simply as a how-to manual for making top-shelf vinegar or vinegar-based recipes. Consider it your guide to unlocking the potential of every sweet, salty, sour, and savory bit in your food. Believe it or not, acidic and sour

foods like vinegar have the ability to open our senses and make our taste buds more sensitive to all the other tastes. At the same time, they also work to bring balance as well as tone down the intensity of overtly bitter and fatty foods.

As a species, we are hardwired to taste sour foods. Some biologists feel that we evolved this ability in order to know if high-energy foods such as fruit were ripe. Unripe fruits don't have the fully developed sugars we need to consume for instant energy. If we can taste their sourness, then we know to wait a little longer before eating them. On the other hand, there are some biologists who believe we developed this ability to warn us of potentially hazardous foods. Some spoiled foods can accumulate organic acids, and some really acidic foods can actually physically harm us. I'll leave it to the scientists to figure out the reason for our ability to taste sour foods, but with either of these concepts, sour takes on a "forbidden fruit" quality.

My working understanding of sour taste is from years of eating and cooking. I remember when my kids were little and just starting to eat solid food. Amelia and I would give them slices of lemon to gnaw on. With each bite, they would pull back from the lemon and intensely pucker their faces. What looked like displeasure would instantly fade into a smile followed by another bite. This got me thinking about how we look to sour foods as a source of pleasure and enjoyment while eating. I mean, what kid doesn't stuff their mouth repeatedly with Sour Patch Kids on a regular basis?

We simply crave sour foods. This is evident in cuisines around the globe. From the Pennsylvania Dutch to the people of Shanxi Province in northern China, sour foods are an instrumental—actually fundamental—part of how we enjoy what we cook and eat. Why else would a fatty grilled sausage virtually beg to be slathered in a boldly tart brown mustard? Sour ingredients just have a natural way of making us happy. As a chef, it's important to be able to craft and manipulate foods in ways that appease the diner. Vinegar makes this possible to do, to create balance in any dish. It's so important that it has literally become the cornerstone of all my cooking.

With all of that being said, let's thank whoever produced that crappy bottle I bought many moons ago. It was the best twenty-nine dollars I ever pissed down the drain.

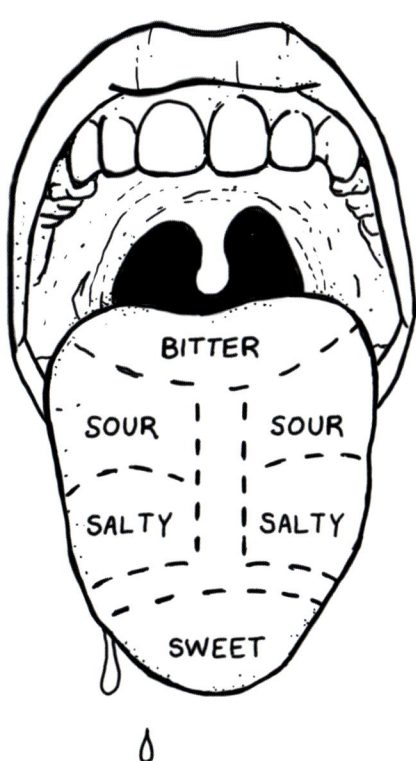

THE POWER OF SOUR

The use of vinegar can have both subtle and major impacts on our food. Using too much or too little can leave you with unintended consequences, so it's important to learn where the sour "Goldilocks zone" is. This can be tricky at first because of the various ways that vinegar reacts with different ingredients and tastes. It's important for you as a chef to understand how all of the tastes work together. For example, if a dish comes off as too sweet, sour and salt will help balance it out. If a dish is too salty or too sour, additional sweet will do the same thing.

This balancing ratio applies to food that is too bitter and needs to be offset by the inclusion of some umami. Vinegar is a great equalizer that'll even out the bitterness. With this book and enough practice, you'll be in the zone every time you cook. Take crudo (see page 139) as a prime example. When making crudo, you rely on an acid to denature the proteins in the seafood and chemically cook it. The acid rearranges the protein in a way that causes it to lose the water molecules that it's wrapped around. When this happens, the texture of the seafood changes. If you use too much acid, then the texture can toughen to a dry, rubbery mouthfeel. The opposite can happen if too little acid is used. Not enough proteins will denature, and you'll be left with a raw, mushy texture. Finding the right balance is key. In the same way, too little or too much acid in the crudo will affect its taste—too little and there won't be the impact of the pleasant sour flavor that you want; too much and it'll be so sour that it's unpalatable. Because of the multifaceted impact that acid has on food, it is a cornerstone of cooking. That makes it extremely powerful and indispensable in the kitchen.

1. THERE ARE MANY WAYS TO MAKE VINEGAR, AND EACH ONE HAS ITS PROS AND CONS.

During my many years of making vinegar, I've settled on two styles that I like best and work consistently for me every time. The first is what I refer to as "scrap vinegars." I chose this name because I first started making these vinegars using the peels, or scraps, from apples. I've since broadened this to include any vinegar I make that needs to go through an alcoholic fermentation before it can ferment into vinegar. This means that I classify the Begonia Vinegar on page 41 to be a scrap vinegar even though I'm not technically using scraps.

The second style of vinegar making that I use are ones that I refer to as "boozy brews." These are vinegars made from alcohol. My Old-School Red Wine Vinegar (page 34) is a prime example. It doesn't rely on me personally going through the process of fermenting grapes into wine and then fermenting the wine into vinegar. I start with a good drinkable wine that I enjoy and allow a vinegar mother to convert it into a great vinegar.

As you'll see, these two methods will allow you to make any vinegar that you could possibly dream up.

2. YOU CAN HAVE TOO HIGH OR TOO LOW OF AN ABV (ALCOHOL BY VOLUME) IN THE BEVERAGE YOU WANT TO TURN INTO VINEGAR.

If the ABV is more than 15 percent, then even the alcohol-loving *Acetobacter* will die off. If the ABV is less than 3 percent, then various types of wild yeasts can start to grow on the surface of the alcohol before the *Acetobacter* establishes itself. This isn't necessarily a safety issue but rather one related to quality. These wild yeasts can create stale, dank, and musty flavors that are unbecoming. On top of that, these yeasts can be attacked and contaminated with molds that may eventually spoil a base liquid. Because of this, I recommend starting a vinegar with alcohol in the 6 to 12 percent ABV range.

This covers most beer and wine that you'll want to use to make vinegar. If you're feeling adventurous and want to ferment a high-ABV wine or spirit, such as a quart of 40 percent tequila or spiced rum, into vinegar, you'll need to dilute it with water. Use this equation to dilute it to 10 percent ABV: $V \times ((S / F)-1) = D$, where V is for *volume*, S is for *starting ABV*, F is for *final ABV*, and D is for how much water you need to *dilute S* with. For example, based on a 40 percent tequila that you're trying to reduce to 10 percent ABV, $1 \times ((^{40}/_{10})-1) = 3$. The *1* in this equation represents the 1 quart of tequila. The *40* represents the starting ABV, and the *10* represents the target ABV. The *3* is the amount of water in quarts that has to be added to the 1 quart of 40 percent ABV tequila to dilute it to 10 percent ABV.

Math isn't my strong suit, but I find this equation ridiculously helpful when I want to ferment a high-alcohol spirit that otherwise is too alcoholic to convert. If you're going to start a vinegar from scratch, then you'll need to ferment the base liquid to the optimal range. You can easily and cheaply purchase, from a home-brew supply store, an instrument called a hydrometer that will measure the level of sugars in a fermenting alcohol. By taking such readings, you can precisely measure the ABV. This works only if you're starting from scratch and if no alcohol is present, like in the Strawberry Wine Vinegar on page 42. You can also take a much simpler approach and just use your taste buds. To do this, you'll need two alcoholic beverages, one of which is at 6 percent ABV and the other at 12 percent ABV; these will be the controls that you taste test your home brew against. If starting from a sugary base liquid that you're first fermenting into alcohol and want to know what the approximate ABV is, taste it, then swish it around your mouth to

let the alcohol settle on your palate. Next, do the same thing with the 6 percent alcoholic beverage. If they taste similar in their alcohol level, then you know that you're around 6 percent ABV. If yours doesn't taste as alcoholic as the control, then add some sugar and let it ferment further. If your home brew tastes stronger than the 6 percent control, then taste it against the 12 percent control. If it's not as strong, then you know you're somewhere in the 8 to 10 percent ABV range. If your home brew is stronger, then add water, a tablespoon at a time, and continue to taste until your brew is similar to the 12 percent control. This may seem unsophisticated, but it is how people measured such things for millennia until the hydrometer was perfected in the eleventh century. I frequently use this taste-test method. If you are starting a vinegar from a low-ABV alcoholic beverage (about 3 percent), such as my Modernist Cucumber Vinegar on page 39, then add a neutral spirit, such as vodka, a tablespoon at a time, until you bring it up to somewhere in the 6 to 12 percent range. You want to use a neutral spirt (like vodka or, if you're able to procure it, moonshine) so that you don't change the final flavor profile of your finished vinegar.

3. VINEGAR NEEDS OXYGEN.

The chemical formula for vinegar reads "ethanol/alcohol (CH_3CH_2OH) and oxygen (O_2)." This is because the *Acetobacter* is technically a living organism, and all living organisms, from great white sharks to duck-billed platypuses to us, need oxygen to survive. Oxygenating your vinegar can be done in one of two ways. The first is the simplest and most low tech: Ferment your vinegar in a vessel that has a wide opening. Anything from a widemouthed mason jar to a five-gallon bucket will work. Just don't use

a necked vessel, such as a wine bottle, as very little of the alcohol will be exposed to atmospheric oxygen. When making vinegar this way, expect it to take anywhere from two to four months. I taste the vinegar every week or so to gauge how it's progressing. When it tastes good to me, I bottle and age it for at least another month or up to several years. The second method is to force oxygen into your alcoholic base. You can easily do so by buying a $15 aquarium pump and running it into your vessel. If you do this, then it won't matter what type of vessel you ferment your vinegar in. This forced oxygenation greatly speeds up the vinegar fermentation, shortening the time it takes to make vinegar to mere weeks. The trade-off is that these vinegars don't have much complexity. They're one-note sour vinegars. If you bottle them and age them for a few months, you'll notice they transform into balanced vinegars that aren't as harsh and develop wonderful fruity, and even savory, notes.

4. FLIES HAPPEN.

If there is food, there are flies. This is one thing that all restaurants around the world battle. All restaurants have flytraps to catch these assholes before they land on the food and potentially wreak havoc. The most effective flytraps are ones that use vinegar as bait. So when making vinegar at home, be prepared to have a few unexpected visitors show up. It's just one of the acceptable compromises to having great vinegar at your disposal. The simple solution? Cheesecloth. Cover your fermenting vinegar tightly with cheesecloth. This will allow atmospheric oxygen to reach the *Acetobacter* while preventing flies from entering. I will say that even with a tight-fitting cheesecloth cover, you're bound to occasionally get a fly or two caught up in your brew. The good but kind of gross thing is that a vinegar with a pH of 4.3 and lower is acidic enough to kill not only the unintended guests but also any pathogenic microbes that the flies may have brought with them (you can buy strips to measure the pH level of your brew from Amazon). Simply strain your finished vinegar through a coffee filter before you bottle and age it.

5. SUGAR MATTERS.

If you're starting from scratch, then you'll need sugar and water (and possibly yeast) to make your alcoholic base liquid. Not all the sugar has to be added; there are plenty of fruits and vegetables that have enough sugars in them that simply putting them into a mason jar and covering them with a little water will be sufficient to start the two-stage vinegar ferment. This is literally what I do when I make an apple scrap vinegar, which I do after I make apple tarte Tatin. I simply take all the apple peels and bits from the cores, put them in a 1-quart widemouthed mason jar, and add enough water to cover them by about an inch. I cover the jar with cheesecloth, put it on top of my fridge, and then wait. Once I see bubbles moving in the jar, I know that the wild yeasts on the apple skins have begun to metabolize (ferment the sugars found in the skins and cores). These bubbles are carbon dioxide, CO_2, and are a by-product of the first stage in the two-stage ferment. Sometimes there's so much CO_2 produced that the top of the jar looks like a bubble bath. It's at this point that I'll taste a spoonful against a 6 percent control and gauge the ABV. If it tastes weak, I'll add a tablespoon of sugar to give the yeast more food to metabolize into alcohol. Typically, about a month into the ferment, this solution is somewhere near an ABV of 6 percent. At this point, I wait and watch again, tasting every other week, until I see a mother of vinegar (a gooey-looking cellulose film that helps turn alcohol into acetic acid and, thus, vinegar) develop on the surface of the ferment. Once this happens, I know that the alcohol that I made has started its second stage of fermentation and begun its transformation into vinegar. Once the mother of vinegar has formed, most of the yeasts that started the alcoholic fermentation will die off and settle to the bottom of the vessel. Any sugars not eaten by the yeast will convert into alcohol and stay around. This can work to your advantage if you want a sweet vinegar like balsamic. I like my apple scrap vinegar to have a hint of sweetness, as it really brings out the fruity flavors of the apples.

6. TIME AND PATIENCE ARE YOUR FRIENDS.

Making vinegar takes time and requires you to be patient. The trade-off is that you really need to invest only a few minutes of actual work into the whole process. The microbes we rely on to ferment the vinegar are the ones that do all the hard work. You just need to make sure you keep them happy.

7. THINK LIKE A MICROBE.

I stated before that even though bacteria are very different from us, they are still living organisms. That being the case, they have, generally speaking, the same basic needs and wants as we do. They want to be in a safe and comfortable environment within which they can go about their business in peace. Just like us, they need oxygen, prefer moderate temperatures in the 70° to 90°F range, and don't like prolonged exposure to direct sunlight. If you meet these needs, they'll work tirelessly around the clock to provide you with the best vinegar you've ever had.

8. THE VARIETY IS INFINITE.

If you can dream of a type of vinegar, then you can make it. I've made vinegar from ingredients as unusual as stinging nettles and prosciutto stock (see page 37) to something as mundane as red wine (see page 34). I've even gotten bottles of dandelion wine from friends and random unlabeled spirits from estate sales that I've fermented into vinegar. As long as there is alcohol present, or the ability to ferment something into alcohol, then you can transform anything into vinegar. Experiment and don't be heartbroken if something doesn't work out.

Vinegar-Making EQUIPMENT

Now that you know how vinegar is made, it's time to stock up on the items that'll actually produce the sour stuff. It's a short list but these instruments are absolutely necessary to have on hand, as they'll help you make the vinegars that are eventually utilized in every recipe in this book. And here's the good news—everything listed is either extremely inexpensive and easily sourced from Amazon of free by picking through your recycling.

Bottle with a Tight-Fitting Lid You can use an old wine bottle, a clasp-top bottle, an old beer bottle, or similar to age and store your finished vinegar.

Cheesecloth This material will keep flies and debris out.

Glass and Food-Grade Containers I've used everything from glass mason jars to five-gallon plastic buckets for fermenting vinegar. Wooden and stainless-steel barrels also work well. Basically, any vessel made out of a material that isn't too porous or reactive will work (reactive materials include cast iron, unlined copper, and aluminum).

Mother While we encourage involving your mom in the process of making vinegar (be a sweetheart for once), this piece of equipment is in reference to the most important thing you'll need. The mother is a disklike, gelatinous shape that will float on the surface of the vinegar. It occurs when the *Acetobacter* form a cellulose raft where they can live. The mother will pick up a color that's reflective of the vinegar that it's growing on, so a red-wine vinegar mother will be red or purple. Mothers can die (but hopefully not your human mother any time soon), so it's important to continually make vinegar to keep yours alive. There are two distinct ways to procure a mother.

Grow a vinegar mother: To make a vinegar mother from scratch, simply put some alcohol (6 to 12 percent ABV) in a 1-quart widemouthed mason jar, cover it with cheesecloth, and let it sit until you see a jellylike disk—the mother—floating on the surface. Once you've produced a mother, pour the contents of the jar into your base liquid (your wine, beer, cider, or other alcohol). From here, your mother will continue to grow indefinitely as long

VINEGAR CHEAT SHEET

When a chemist looks at vinegar, they see $CH_3CH_2OH + O_2 \rightarrow CH_3COOH + H_2O$, or the conversion of ethanol/alcohol (CH_3CH_2OH) and oxygen (O_2) to acetic acid (CH_3COOH) and water (H_2O). I don't know about you, but this just isn't something that I can wrap my brain around. What I can understand is that a genus of bacteria named *Acetobacter* literally eats and metabolizes alcohol into a mixture of acetic acid and water that we've named *vinegar*. The name we've given to this metabolic process is *fermentation*. I mentioned earlier that winemakers have literally been trying to prevent their alcohol from turning into vinegar for millennia. This is partly because *Acetobacter* bacteria are everywhere. They're on our skin, on the foods we eat, even floating in the very air we breathe. They're so common that any alcoholic beverage with a tolerable measure of alcohol by volume (ABV), when left out and exposed to air, will eventually ferment into vinegar seemingly on its own. Vinegar is what we call a two-stage ferment. This means that you first have to allow yeast to ferment a sugary liquid into alcohol and then allow the *Acetobacter* to ferment the alcohol into vinegar. Vinegar is literally a fermented ferment. How's that for a mind fuck? I've provided recipes in chapter 1 that walk you through making vinegar from scratch as well as start at the second stage of fermentation.

as there is alcohol for it to consume. If you need to take a break from vinegar making, store your mother in a closed jar, making sure to open the jar and leave it uncovered at room temperature for a couple of hours every week. This will allow enough oxygen to enter the jar to keep the vinegar mother alive until you're ready to use it again.

Seek a vinegar mother: Ask a vinegar-freak friend for some of his/her mother. From my personal experience, there are numerous Internet-based fermentation forums where users will gladly gift you a mother if you ask. WildFermentation.com is a great place to start your search. Or, you can go to eBay or Etsy and search for retailers or suppliers who will sell you one.

pH Test Strips or an Inexpensive pH Meter
If you want to know the exact pH of your vinegar, then get some pH test strips or a meter. However, these things aren't entirely necessary unless you intend to develop a vinegar to make and sell.

THE THIRTEEN COMMANDMENTS OF *Vinegar Making*

I

DON'T. BE. AFRAID.

Not to copy Nike's mantra, but it is this simple: Just do it. Make vinegar as you would any other pursuit that you pour your entire heart into. Then go nuts with the results. Have a recipe that requires citrus? Substitute vinegar. Want to punch up a salad dressing? Toss in some vinegar. Need to make that cocktail extra-funky? Employ a white wine vinegar or coffee–stout beer vinegar for an extra kick. Embrace the freaking sour.

II

CHECK YOUR LEVEL OF COMMITMENT

In order to become a vinegar-maker, you're committing yourself with time and money, so ask yourself before you brew, how far am I willing to go with this?

III

GOOD VINEGAR DOES NOT HAVE TO BE EXPENSIVE

You don't have to spend an arm and a leg to get the vinegary push you need to send a recipe over the top. Purchasing great aged vinegars tends to be expensive, meaning you won't typically find a bottle that's more than a year old for less than twenty dollars. Such types of vinegars typically require refrigeration after opening to maintain freshness and have born-on dates stating when the base liquid was made, when it was bottled, and how long it was aged. When you make your own, you can bypass all that.

IV

SOURCE CONSCIOUSLY

Quality matters. Wear it like your favorite baseball team's fitted hat and be prideful of the vinegars you're using. When you read the label for vinegar, ideally the fewer the ingredients, the better. If you see sugar, caramel color, or sulfites, run. Your vinegar should include a base vinegar liquid (like red wine or beer), a little bit of water, and a vinegar mother. That's all you need.

V

CONSIDER YOUR USE

Not all vinegars are created equal. Assuming they're not garbage, all vinegars will lead you to sour-infused greatness, but keep in mind the foods they accompany and how you are using them. I've got a three-tiered rating system that details the types of vinegars and how to use them.

Gold-Level Vinegar This is your "top-shelf" finishing vinegar. It'll be something like a twenty-five- or thirty-year-old balsamic or sherry vinegar. You do not want to cook with this vinegar. I recommend only drizzling it on foods such as vanilla ice cream, strawberries, or cheese.

Silver-Level Vinegar This is a midlevel base vinegar that you'll use to dress a salad. Think of your good red wine vinegar, generic cider vinegar, malt vinegar, and so on. You can also throw one of these vinegars into a cocktail or drizzle fries with the aforementioned malt vinegar.

Bronze-Level Vinegar This is your bottom-rung utility (but not crap) vinegar that'll be a distilled vinegar. Use it for pickling and poaching food.

VI

VINEGAR IS THE OG ACID

Long before we utilized other acids in cooking (as lemons, limes, and oranges were an extreme luxury in ancient times), we had vinegar. While this commandment has no practical use, know that nothing touches vinegar when it comes to imbuing acidity in a food.

VII

SCREW OTHERS' OPINIONS

If you like what you've made, use it. For example, Southern chef Sean Brock uses a Mountain Dew–based vinegar at his legendary Charleston, South Carolina, restaurant, McCrady's Tavern. It's an outside-the-box use of a mass-produced soda, but it works. Flex your creative thinking and do something nuts. Try to answer the question "Does it vinegar?" for everything.

VIII

SALT-AND-VINEGAR CHIPS ARE PERFECT

The potency of the salt-and-vinegar combination proves how vinegar, with the help of salt, can turn even a mundane food item like potatoes into a gloriously edible concoction. Seriously.

IX

LOCATION MATTERS

Much like growing grapes to make wine, your *terroir* (the ground and atmosphere from which you're getting your vinegar's ingredients) has a huge impact on how your vinegar will turn out. Here in northeastern Ohio, apples are king; therefore, we're going to be able to make primo apple cider vinegar; frankly, better than anywhere else in America. Out West, especially in California, wine-based vinegars are king. And if you're at all familiar with the vinegar-based barbecue of the Carolinas, distilled (aka white) vinegars are your best bet. Distilled white vinegars are ones made from neutral distilled spirits such as moonshine or vodka. The vinegar itself is not distilled.

X

NEVER FORGET THE FORMULA

The extremely easy way to remember how vinegar is made is the following equation:

Juice + Mother + Air + Time = Vinegar

Tattoo that shit on your arm if you need to commit it to memory.

XI

BALANCE, BALANCE, BALANCE!

Vinegar is at its best when it hits all your taste buds. While we remember ketchup for its sugary potency (because of the commonly used recipe for mass-produced versions), expertly made ketchup (see pages 78 and 80) is a flavor bomb that nukes all your flavor receptors, leaving every part of your tongue satisfied.

XII

USE IT LITERALLY EVERYWHERE

After you've conquered a batch, use it on everything from fries to the insides of crepe cakes. As we'll prove in this book, vinegar is as omnipotent as the salt shaker sitting on your table—and a bottle of it deserves a place next to that shaker.

XIII

VINEGAR IS IMMORTAL

Once you've turned your juice of choice into vinegar, it'll stay vinegar. There's no going back, bro. It'll be a vinegar *forever*. That's pretty cool.

CHEF'S NOTES ON
Proper Ingredients

One of the things my restaurant staffs and I pride ourselves on is ensuring that every meal features the finest locally sourced ingredients we can purchase. Whether it's an excellent piece of pork shoulder or superb vegetables, each dish we put on a table only includes the best. But I know that not every home cook will have the same ability (or budget) to procure items like we do.

Because of this reality, I've highlighted, identified, and broken down several foods that will require special attention in multiple recipes throughout this book, including dairy, oil, mirepoix, bread crumbs, beef, and fish. Maybe you don't have the time or budget to serve the absolute best of everything, but these are the places where your schedule and money can make a big impact on what you eat. It's not an exhaustive list; it's my list. I hope it inspires you to better your cooking as you continue your culinary adventures.

WHY DAIRY AND EGGS MATTER

Just as you'll see later on, sourcing the best-quality and environmentally sound ingredients are of the upmost importance to me as a chef. It's a fact that cows raised primarily on grass yield better-tasting dairy products, such as butter, cheese, milk, and yogurt. I recommend grass-fed dairy products for all of the recipes in this book; however, it's still a free country, so make your own choices. Here, I break down my guidelines to selecting butter, eggs, and milk, the key building blocks to many recipes throughout this book.

Butter Butter is the solid fats that are separated from cream after churning. Just by agitating the cream, all the fats cling to one another, which gives you butter. To be called *butter*, it must be 80 percent or more butterfat by weight. Typical high-quality butters start at 84 percent butterfat; if you're shopping for bargain butter, pay attention to the butterfat. Also, keep in mind that butter absorbs the scent of whatever is around it. Don't keep your butter near, say, fish if you don't want it to end up tasting like fish. Be cognizant of how you store it.

Cultured vs. Uncultured Cultured butter just tastes better. Widely available in America, it's a traditional step of butter preservation from olden times that yields typically higher butterfat and higher lactic acid content (meaning, it tastes better and works wonders for your digestive system). In this cookbook, I frequently use cultured butter when I want a tangy, buttery flavor to stand out.

Salted vs. Unsalted I typically choose salted butter for almost every recipe because I feel it helps keep the flavor and aroma of the butter, which produces a more intense, buttery experience in the final dish.

Eggs At the end of the day, eggs are flavored by four things—freshness, breed of chicken, feed of chicken, and environment. Hens that eat a range of insects, grasses, seeds, and berries yield typically higher-quality, better-tasting eggs. But if your chicken eats only corn and lives in a cage, surrounded by other chickens in cages, you won't receive a very consistent, flavorful egg. Like grass-fed dairy, we recommend that all recipes in this book that require eggs utilize good eggs from pasture-raised chickens.

Milk You want to buy whole milk, anywhere from 3 to 4 percent butterfat, because it produces better flavor in your end product. Live by this cardinal rule: Fatty things are delicious.

WHY THE QUALITY OF YOUR OIL MATTERS

First and foremost, when it comes to imported oils, there is a lot of counterfeiting and deception. It's crucial to source your oil from a trusted manufacturer that has a lot of turnover of its product—and this is especially true of olive oil. Why? Like the old restaurant adages *Don't order fish on Mondays* and *The busier food trucks have better food*, you can ascertain that an oil-maker is quality when they sell so much that they constantly have only fresh ingredients on hand—nothing's old.

The younger the oil, the fresher it is; the older an oil, the greater the chance that it'll spoil. Unfortunately, most of the oil we're used to cooking with is actually spoiled oil (it's akin to how Starbucks has convinced everyone that the flavor of burnt, over-roasted coffee is the gold standard). The only thing you can look for in the store to prevent purchasing something rancid is to check the born-on date. If something is older than a year, be wary. When you get home, you can also smell it. If the oil smells sweet or sour, then it's bad. The main factor that should determine your purchase should be the born-on date as opposed to the expiration date (and if you're going to spend more than twenty dollars on a bottle, it's imperative that it includes a born-on date). Following are the oil terms we use in recipes in the book.

Blended Oil For us, this would be a mix of a highly flavored oil, such as olive oil, and a neutral oil. The goal is to get some of the flavor of the olive oil with a higher smoke point at a lower cost. (The smoke point is the temperature at which oil starts to smoke and potentially burn and combust, developing burnt and unpleasant flavors in the food.) We use at least 50 percent neutral oil in our blends, but it comes down to your personal preference. If you want to do 75 percent neutral oil and 25 percent olive oil, then knock yourself out. In my restaurants, we blend our own oil, mainly to control the quality.

Neutral Oil Neutral oil is any oil that does not have a distinct taste and allows the flavor of produce to come through clearly. I recommend using a high-end grapeseed or a non-GMO canola oil.

Olive Oil It's superhealthful and delicious, and olive oil is multipurpose. It works just as well as a garnish as it does for cooking. Here are my breakdown of grades of olive oil.

"Gold Standard" Your highest-tier olive oil will be single origin, estate produced, and synonymous with cold-pressed extra-virgin oils. These are oils that are produced with one type of olive by one type of grower. Most often, these oils are used when they're young, as garnish or on salads. It's not until they're older (more than a year) that you should start cooking with them. They tend to be very expensive, and you have to order them directly from the producer. I recommend getting these oils from Olio Verde or Casa Caponetti in Italy.

"Silver Standard" The next tier would be midrange oils that are very versatile. They're flavorful enough that they could work as a garnish, but they're not too delicate to use for cooking. These are general purpose and still of good quality. In my mind, a lot of domestic oils fall into this category. Two classifications used for such oils are *old extra-virgin oils* and oils labeled as just *virgin oil*.

I recommend getting these from your general grocery store. They don't have to be too expensive but shouldn't be too cheap either (they should be just less than twenty dollars).

"Bronze Standard" These are often labeled simply as *olive oil* and are the worst of the worst. I would use these only if I were on a camping trip in the middle of nowhere and it was the only thing on the shelf at the local gas station. They're not even fit for deep-frying. In their place, I'll use a blended oil instead.

WHY YOU SHOULD SWEAR BY MIREPOIX

Mirepoix is a mixture of aromatic vegetables used to flavor a stock or a sauce. It may sound French and fancy, but it's nothing to be afraid of. It's the aromatics that form a basis for a cuisine, a holy trinity in most cases (case in point, France, where it's celery, carrots, and onions). Throughout the book, we'll call for several different forms of mirepoix, which you'll find here.

Cajun Trinity This uses green bell pepper, onion, and celery. You really don't find this kind used outside New Orleans and Cajun cuisine. For the record, none of our recipes will call for it directly, but it can be used in place of many mirepoix examples in the book. Feel free to switch it in at your digression when we call for mirepoix.

Salad Mirepoix This mixture can include whatever kitchen vegetable you have around and like—carrot, celery root, celery, shallot, radish, and so on. You'll use this in Red Wine–Braised Lentils & Frisée Salad Dijon (page 93), Brined Beer-Can Chicken (page 121), Bone-In Beef Pot Roast (page 130), and Brined & Boiled Corned Lamb & Cabbage (page 124).

Sofrito In Spain, Portugal, Italy, and Latin American countries, this will typically include a mixture of peppers, onions, and carrot, and sometimes cilantro and garlic. Sofrito in northern Italy includes the classic three—onions, carrots, and celery—plus pancetta and garlic, run through a meat grinder.

Southeast Asian This uses garlic, ginger, and scallion. We use this blend in the XO à la Trentina recipe on page 112, and it tastes *[Homer Simpson drool face]* good.

Stock Mirepoix This is the classical composition of onion, carrot, and celery. It appears in the Sunday Gravy over Cavatelli on page 135.

SALAD

STOCK

SOFRITO

SOUTHEAST ASIAN

WHY GRASS-FED AND AGED BEEF IS BEST

For beef, we choose Ohio-born-and-raised certified Angus beef, reared in pastures on grass. One hundred percent pasture-fed beef is more delicious but more expensive; however, buy it if you can afford it. Good examples of this type of beef include A5 Miyazaki Wagyu or Tuscan-style Chianina beef. Pasture-raised beef is the most environmentally sound option, as well as being better for your health and the overall taste of your dish. Any price difference that you see at the market is more than worth spending because of these three additional benefits. Also, aged beef is great, too! Don't let older cuts scare you off. The more time it has under its belt, the better it gets. Ideally, our steaks dry-age for twenty days, but we've gone as long as one hundred days. We suggest going directly to your local butcher because he or she specializes in meat and knows the ins and outs of every cut. Have your butcher seam out all connective tissue ("seaming" is a way of butchering meat that separates individual muscles from each other; the place where two muscles meet is a seam), silver skin (a thin silvery covering of connective tissue found on cuts of meat), and interior fat from the steaks. But ask him or her to save all the trim and scraps for you (these pieces are good to render down so that you have animal fat to cook and fry in; they're also great for fortifying or making stock). If your steak is already cut or you're buying it wrapped in plastic on top of Styrofoam, then purchase some stew meat or scraps to have handy for making sauces or stock.

WHY GOOD FISH MATTERS

It's crucial to select the proper fish in order to not only serve the best dish possible but also to make environmentally sound choices. You can find the most up-to-date information on domestic and international fish on the Seafood Watch app from Monterey Bay Aquarium (it's easily found within the Apple and Google Play stores). When I cook and I need a general cut of fish, I default to halibut. If halibut's not available, then I make sure to use farm-raised sturgeon or wild black cod.

HOW TO CREATE THE PERFECT BREAD CRUMBS

1 cup cubed day-old bread (heels, centers, white, wheat . . . whatevs)

1 tablespoon "gold standard" olive oil (see page 23)

2 tablespoons fines herbes (see page 232)

1 teaspoon kosher salt

1 tablespoon salted butter, melted

Several times throughout the book I ask you to make bread crumbs for your dish. Instead of bogging down the recipes that require the accoutrement, I've described the entire process here. Commit it to memory (also, use it for all of your future cooking excursions that require bread crumbs).

1 Preheat the oven to 350°F.

2 Put the cubed bread into a food processor, add the olive oil, fines herbes, salt, and butter. Pulse a couple times to combine. Spread out the mixture on a baking sheet.

3 Bake until the crumbs take on a deep, rich, toasted brown color, about 20 minutes. Let the bread crumbs cool completely before using. Store in an airtight container, at room temperature, for up to 3 days.

1
VINEGARS

About eight years ago, I got to speak with one of my favorite wine-makers, John Kongsgaard. If you're not familiar with John, whose nickname is "Nature Boy," he likes to take the natural approach that many Californian vintners swear by, championing their weather, soil, grapes, and Chardonnay for being totally badass. In terms of process, he always has primo grapes and presses them pristinely before placing them in barrels to sit.

I found myself explaining to him and his son how I make vinegar. To give you a sense of the scenery, John, who's tall and bearded—this distinguished human being—is stroking his white scruff and furrowing his brow. Eventually, he stops me, looks me dead in the eye, and says, "So everything that I'm naturally trying to stop the wine from doing, you're trying to get the wine to do?" His comment stopped me dead in my tracks. It wasn't a way to conceive of vinegar making that I'd considered before, but it was pretty much true.

When I was an amateur vinegar-maker, I simply thought that I was transforming this liquid into vinegar; however, John's viewpoint was *No, no, that liquid is going to be vinegar at some point no matter what you do*. It didn't necessarily change a lot of what we did, but it helped me understand the process by thinking about it in reverse. I'm making vinegar in the same way that the best vintners make wine, just ushering the process along a bit more quickly. Whoa.

Now, we're ready to put you on the path to becoming a master vinegar- and winemaker like John, exploring my favorite vinegars to produce. All of these vinegars will be featured in various recipes in this book, so keep an eye out for their inclusion. While we explain the background behind the processes that go into each vinegar recipe, you can find full explanations behind how certain vinegars are made in "Vinegar IRL" on page 7.

GREENHOUSE TAVERN-STYLE CRAFT-BEER VINEGAR

Makes about 1 quart

EQUIPMENT

1-quart widemouthed glass container

Large spoon

Cheesecloth or paper towel

Rubber band or butcher's twine

pH test strips (optional)

INGREDIENTS

4 cups beer

Turning beer into vinegar is an ancient tradition, but we can thank the British for popularizing it. While most of Europe was focused on making wine and wine vinegars, the British were brewing beer and making beer vinegars. You're probably familiar with these types of vinegars by their more common name: malt vinegar. You know, the one that you sprinkle on fish and chips. Once I owned my own restaurant, Greenhouse Tavern, which held hundreds of feet of drafts lines, it was only natural to begin mass-producing premium craft-beer vinegars. This recipe cemented my sour legacy.

When you begin making this vinegar, you'll want to keep in mind something important. After you mix everything together and as time goes on, you'll notice a layer of what looks like gelatin growing on the surface. This is the mother of vinegar (see page 13). Without it, the alcohol won't be converted into vinegar.

Make sure to use a beer for this that is 6 to 12 percent alcohol by volume (ABV). And don't use one that is too hoppy, or your vinegar will be bitter.

1. Wash the glass container in hot, soapy water, then rinse and dry thoroughly.

2. Pour the beer into the container. Stir with the spoon to dissipate the carbonation, and then let sit for 30 minutes. You want the beer to be flat and not fizzy.

3. Cover the container's opening with cheesecloth, securing it with a rubber band, to keep out debris.

4. Let the container sit in a cool, dry, and dark place for 2 weeks. Then, give the mixture a taste; if it's sharp, tangy, and sour (like other vinegars you've had), it's now vinegar (It's perfectly okay to taste; no pathogens can survive in either the alcohol or the vinegar.) If you prefer, you can also judge the progress of your vinegar by using pH strips; we shoot for a reading of 4 or below on the pH scale (see page 234).

NOTE When you first taste the mixture, if it *doesn't* taste like vinegar, that means it either needs more time, oxygen, or alcohol, or a combination of the three. Let it sit for another week and then taste again. If there has been no further change, add a shot of vodka to the ferment in order to feed the mother and wait another week to taste once more. Remember that some vinegars develop very hot profiles while others are mellow; an infinite amount of variables contribute to this.

OLD-SCHOOL RED WINE VINEGAR

Makes about 1 quart

EQUIPMENT

1-quart widemouthed glass container

Cheesecloth or paper towel

Rubber band or butcher's twine

pH test strips (optional)

INGREDIENTS

One 750-ml bottle red wine, 6% to 12% ABV (see page 7), the best that you can afford

For millennia, winemakers struggled with what they thought was a problem: How to keep their wine from turning into vinegar. What was, and still is, a problem for winemakers is a gift to a vinegar geek like me. I always add a year of aging to the vinegar to achieve a deep and bold flavor. One rule to always follow is to use outstanding wine. The better the wine, the better the vinegar.

Save the wine bottle and cork and use them to bottle and age your vinegar.

1. Wash the glass container in hot, soapy water, then rinse and dry thoroughly.

2. Pour the wine into the container. Cover the container's opening with cheesecloth, securing it with a rubber band, to keep out debris.

3. Let the container sit in a cool, dry, and dark place for 2 weeks. Then, give the wine a taste; if it's sharp, tangy, and sour (like other vinegars you've had), it's now vinegar. (It's perfectly okay to taste; no pathogens can survive in either the alcohol or the vinegar.) If you prefer, you can also judge the progress of your vinegar by using pH strips; we shoot for a reading of 4 or below on the pH scale (see page 234).

VARIATION You can actually make any type of white wine vinegar, champagne vinegar, sherry vinegar, or rice vinegar with this method by starting with the appropriate wine, champagne, sherry, or sake.

APPLE CIDER VINEGAR

Makes about 1 quart

EQUIPMENT

1-quart widemouthed glass container

Large spoon

Cheesecloth or paper towel

Rubber band or butcher's twine

pH test strips (optional)

INGREDIENTS

4 cups microbrewed hard cider

Apple cider vinegars are extremely easy to create and versatile to cook with, making them one of the most widely consumed vinegars. They're also intensely American, as they were a result of Johnny Appleseed giving apple seeds and seedlings to settlers as they traveled west across the country. The resulting bitter apples were perfect for cider, which made for good vinegar. Make sure the cider is between 6 and 12 percent ABV; and it shouldn't include extra flavorings, or the vinegar will be flavored similarly.

1 Wash the glass container in hot, soapy water, then rinse and dry thoroughly.

2 Pour the cider into the container. Stir with the spoon to dissipate the carbonation, and then let sit for 30 minutes. You want the cider to be flat and not fizzy.

3 Cover the container's opening with cheesecloth, securing it with a rubber band, to keep out debris.

4 Let the container sit in a cool, dry, and dark place for 2 weeks. Then, give the cider a taste; if it's sharp, tangy, and sour (like other vinegars you've had), it's now vinegar. (It's perfectly okay to taste; no pathogens can survive in either the alcohol or the vinegar.) If you prefer, you can also judge the progress of your vinegar by using pH strips; we shoot for a reading of 4 or below on the pH scale (see page 234).

APPLE WINE VINEGAR

Makes about 1 quart

EQUIPMENT

1-quart widemouthed glass container

Large bowl

Cheesecloth or paper towel

Rubber band or butcher's twine

pH test strips (optional)

INGREDIENTS

4 cups filtered clarified apple juice

2 tablespoons sugar

Apfelwein essig, apple wine vinegar, is like a champagne vinegar in its body and its palate, producing a distinctly bright and crisp flavor. Made famous by Gegenbauer, one of Europe's most acclaimed artisans, it is a revelation that many young culinarians cannot express in words when they first try it. The big difference between apple *wine* vinegar and apple *cider* vinegar is that apple wine vinegar is made from filtered and clarified apple juice, making it the perfect addition to a nightcap cocktail (see page 226).

1. Wash the glass container in hot, soapy water, then rinse and dry thoroughly.

2. In the large bowl, combine the apple juice and sugar, stirring until the sugar is completely dissolved.

3. Pour the apple juice into the container. Cover the container's opening with cheesecloth, securing it with a rubber band, to keep out debris.

4. Let the container sit in a cool, dry, and dark place for 3 weeks. Then, give the juice a taste; if it's sharp, tangy, and sour (like other vinegars you've had), it's now vinegar. (It's perfectly okay to taste; no pathogens can survive in either the alcohol or the vinegar.) If you prefer, you can also judge the progress of your vinegar by using pH strips; we shoot for a reading of 4 or below on the pH scale (see page 234).

PROSCIUTTO-SCOTCH VINEGAR

Makes about 1 quart

EQUIPMENT

Large saucepan

Two 1-quart widemouthed glass containers

Large bowl

Cheesecloth or paper towel

Rubber band or butcher's twine

pH test strips (optional)

INGREDIENTS

8 ounces prosciutto scraps

1 quart cold water

1 cup best-quality Scotch (preferably Lagavulin 16-year-old Islay Single Malt Scotch Whisky)

This is a vinegar that will really induce a childlike state of awe. It's smoky and full of umami, and it has all the nuance of a great Scotch. The recipe starts by using prosciutto scraps (which you can find easily anywhere prosciutto is sold; just ask the deli worker) to make a stock, which is then used to dilute some Lagavulin Scotch so that it'll ferment into vinegar. I like to sprinkle this on some fresh figs and arugula and eat it with thin slices of prosciutto.

1 In the large saucepan over medium heat, combine the prosciutto scraps and cold water. Bring to a simmer and let simmer for 10 minutes. Strain the resulting stock and discard the prosciutto scraps. Put the stock, uncovered, in the refrigerator to cool completely. Once the stock has cooled, the fat will form a solid layer on the top. Remove the fat and discard it. It is very important to remove the fat that is present in the stock; we don't want it in our vinegar.

2 Wash the glass containers in hot, soapy water, then rinse and dry thoroughly.

3 In the large bowl, combine the stock and Scotch, stirring to mix.

4 Evenly divide the mixture among the containers. Cover the containers' openings with cheesecloth, securing it with a rubber band, to keep out debris.

5 Let the containers sit in a cool, dry, and dark place for 3 to 6 weeks. Then, give the mixture a taste; if it's sharp, tangy, and sour (like other vinegars you've had), it's now vinegar. (It's perfectly okay to taste; no pathogens can survive in either the alcohol or the vinegar.) If you prefer, you can also judge the progress of your vinegar by using pH strips; we shoot for a reading of 4 or below on the pH scale (see page 234).

MODERNIST CUCUMBER VINEGAR

Makes about 1 quart

EQUIPMENT

1-quart widemouthed glass container

Cheesecloth or paper towel

Rubber band or butcher's twine

pH test strips (optional)

INGREDIENTS

3 cups cucumber juice

1 cup 40% ABV vodka

The game here is not to allow the cucumber juice to ferment into cucumber wine; we add some neutral vodka to prevent this from happening. By adding alcohol to the cucumber juice, we give the *Acetobacter* bacteria the food they need to produce vinegar. The resulting vinegar will taste more like a tangy cucumber juice than cucumber beer vinegar (which just sounds gross).

For this recipe, you'll need freshly squeezed cucumber juice. One cucumber should yield about 1 cup of juice. If you have a juicer, use it; if you don't, you can process the peeled cucumbers in a blender and strain the puree through a strainer and coffee filter; discard the pulp and proceed with the recipe.

1 Wash the glass container in hot soapy water, then rinse and dry thoroughly.

2 Pour the cucumber juice and vodka into the container. Cover the container's opening with cheesecloth, securing it with a rubber band, to keep out debris.

3 Let the container sit in a cool, dry, and dark place for 2 weeks. Then, give the mixture a taste; if it's sharp, tangy, and sour (like other vinegars you've had), it's now vinegar. (It's perfectly okay to taste; no pathogens can survive in either the alcohol or the vinegar.) If you prefer, you also can judge the progress of your vinegar by using pH strips; we shoot for a reading of 4 or below on the pH scale (see page 234).

CREAM SODA VINEGAR

Makes about 1 quart

EQUIPMENT

1-quart widemouthed glass container

Large spoon

Cheesecloth or paper towel

Rubber band or butcher's twine

pH test strips (optional)

INGREDIENTS

2½ cups cream soda (such as Old City Soda)

1½ cups vanilla schnapps (such as Dr. McGillicuddy's)

For some reason, which I can't comprehend, cream soda has fallen out of favor in recent times. This is a damn shame. It's so refreshing, crisp, and soothing, especially on a hot summer day. About two years ago, we had a canister of cream soda at the Greenhouse Tavern that had gone flat. I brought it over to Jeremy Umansky, the larder master at my Italian restaurant Trentina, to see what he could do with it, and this vinegar was born. It ends up a fairly sweet vinegar, so it's great simply drizzled on vanilla ice cream, but we recommend using it in the Crispy Ohio Pork (Not) Belly recipe on page 169.

1 Wash the glass container in hot, soapy water, then rinse and dry thoroughly.

2 Pour the cream soda into the container. Stir with the spoon to dissipate the carbonation, and then let sit for 30 minutes. You want the soda to be flat and not fizzy.

3 Once the cream soda is flat, add the schnapps and stir to combine. Cover the container's opening with cheesecloth, securing it with a rubber band, to keep out debris.

4 Let the container sit in a cool, dry, and dark place for 2 weeks. Then, give the mixture a taste; if it's sweet as well as sharp, tangy, and sour (like other vinegars you've had), it's now vinegar. (It's perfectly okay to taste; no pathogens can survive in either the alcohol or the vinegar.) If you prefer, you can also judge the progress of your vinegar by using pH strips; we shoot for a reading of 4 or below on the pH scale (see page 234).

BEGONIA VINEGAR

Makes about 1 quart

EQUIPMENT

2-quart widemouthed glass container

Cheesecloth or paper towel

Rubber band or butcher's twine

pH test strips (optional)

INGREDIENTS

1 pound thoroughly cleaned, certified-organic begonia flowers

One 750-ml bottle Cantina Tramin Gewürztraminer, 6% to 12% ABV (see page 7)

Begonia flowers are beautiful. They're also quite delicious. I got hip to them a few years ago when one of our local farmers started selling them as an edible garnish. They taste intensely sharp due to oxalic acid, the compound that makes both rhubarb and sorrel taste tart. I wanted to capture their beauty in a way that would enable us to have them on hand year-round and not just during the summer. This vinegar will take on a stunning red color if you use red begonias. You can easily grow enough begonias in your yard to yield the 1 pound of blossoms that this recipe calls for. And this vinegar makes for a great addition to the Fried & Marinated Lake Fish in Saor on page 142.

1   Wash the glass container in hot, soapy water, then rinse and dry thoroughly.

2   Using your hands, gently bruise the begonias and then place them in the container.

3   Pour the Gewürztraminer over the flowers. Cover the containers' opening with cheesecloth, securing it with a rubber band, to keep out debris.

4   Let the container sit in a cool, dry, and dark place for 2 weeks. Then, give the mixture a taste; if it's sweet as well as sharp, tangy, and sour (like other vinegars you've had), it's now vinegar. (It's perfectly okay to taste; no pathogens can survive in either the alcohol or the vinegar.) If you prefer, you can also judge the progress of your vinegar by using pH strips; we shoot for a reading of 4 or below on the pH scale (see page 234).

STRAWBERRY WINE VINEGAR

Makes about 2 quarts

EQUIPMENT

1-gallon widemouthed glass container

Large metal bowl

Cheesecloth or paper towel

Rubber band or butcher's twine

pH test strips (optional)

INGREDIENTS

8 pints fresh, ripe, in-season strawberries, washed, hulled, and chopped

¼ cup sugar

This is my favorite way to make vinegar due to my fascination with the process of not using alcohol. You start with just strawberries and a little bit of sugar and let the berries and their naturally occurring yeast ferment into wine, and then allow that wine to convert into vinegar. That's an amazing transformation. This will not taste like a gimmicky strawberry-infused vinegar that you find at a "gourmet" store; it will taste like a full-bodied, intensely flavored, tart strawberry wine vinegar. It's the perfect way to bring a bit of summery strawberry sunshine to a cold and dreary winter day.

1. Wash the glass container in hot, soapy water, then rinse and dry thoroughly.

2. Place the strawberries in the bowl, sprinkle them with the sugar, and mix them well.

3. Put strawberries into the container. Cover the container's opening with cheesecloth, securing it with a rubber band, to keep out debris.

4. Let the container sit in a cool, dry, and dark place for 3 weeks. Then, give the mixture a taste; if it's sharp, tangy, and sour (like other vinegars you've had), it's now vinegar. (It's perfectly okay to taste; no pathogens can survive in either the alcohol or the vinegar.) If you prefer, you can also judge the progress of your vinegar by using pH strips; we shoot for a reading of 4 or below on the pH scale (see page 234).

UMAMI-INFUSED VINEGAR

Makes about 1 gallon

EQUIPMENT

Small mixing bowl

6-quart stockpot

Instant-read thermometer

Fine-mesh strainer

Large bowl

INGREDIENTS

1 cup diced dried mushrooms (any type will work)

1 cup diced dry-packed sun-dried tomato

1 gallon white wine vinegar (see variation, page 34)

2 cups medium-diced Parmesan rinds

2 cups diced country ham or prosciutto

1 cup fish sauce

2 tablespoons liquid Maggi Seasoning

½ cup chopped smoked almonds

2 heads black garlic

2 tablespoons toasted sesame seeds

1 tablespoon dashi powder

As a naturally occurring flavor, umami is a taste element that is savory, delicious, and as addictive as crack. For any culinarian who is into it, it can luckily be finagled, in different ways, into dishes that might not organically contain it, such as with synthetic monosodium glutamate (MSG), or naturally added through the use of roasted tomatoes, Parmesan cheese, and seaweed, among others. This recipe is almost like cheating because it introduces so much umami to a dish. Feel free to remove any of the listed ingredients should they not suit your tastes.

1 In the mixing bowl, combine the dried mushrooms and sun-dried tomatoes and cover with hot water. Allow to reconstitute for 10 minutes.

2 In the stockpot over medium-high heat, combine the reconstituted mushrooms and tomatoes, soaking liquid, vinegar, Parmesan rinds, ham, fish sauce, Maggi Seasoning, almonds, garlic, sesame seeds, and dashi. Bring to a simmer, stirring frequently, then turn the heat to very low and keep the temperature below 200°F on the instant-read thermometer.

3 Allow the mixture to infuse for 2 hours, then remove from the heat and allow to cool overnight at room temperature. Pour through the strainer into a large bowl, transfer to the original vinegar container, and re-cap. Store in a cool, dry, and dark place indefinitely.

DAILY VINEGAR TINCTURE

Makes about 2 ounces

1 tablespoon live active local vinegar

½ tablespoon raw local honey

1 ounce kombucha or water kefir (optional)

The daily tincture is a time-tested remedy to alleviate whatever seasonal allergies might ail you. The wild essence of the honey mixed with a regional vinegar will help build your tolerance to local allergens. A locally produced vinegar will include ingredients made with beneficial microbes from your geographic area; these local microbes are the ones that will benefit you, as opposed to those from a different geographic area. This drink will have your back the next time ragweed blooms in the spring.

In a small bowl, combine the vinegar, honey, and kombucha (if using) and stir to mix. Pour into a shot glass, and shoot.

2
PICKLES

Going back two generations, nobody would've ever thought to *buy* a pickle. It was always something that you made at home because pickling is a preservation technique. If ma and pa had an abundant bounty from the garden or leftover smelts from last night's dinner, they tossed those pieces into some pickling liquid and mason jars. A couple of weeks later, they'd have another round of food. If vinegar-making produces liquids that act as nature's preservatives, then pickling takes the process one step further to ensure that an array of food items can stand the test of time.

The capitalists at Vlassic and other food companies (and nowadays those kimchi-humping hipsters) essentially destroyed this tradition in America. You can buy whatever pickle you want—you no longer have to put any thought into your food. When this happened, all of our ancient, sacred knowledge of pickling and fermenting was pushed aside, and a whole generation of people is currently afraid to ferment and pickle at home.

Things that we're now told are really bad in our food, such as mold, yeast, and bacteria, are the ones responsible for fermenting food and making pickles. I learned early on in my career how beneficial these things were to the foods I wanted to create. I embraced mold and bacteria and found ways to incorporate fermentation into the foods that I was producing. Pickling and fermenting are very straightforward processes. Once you get over the fear of the unknown, you'll want to pickle and ferment everything—from the classic cucumber to crispy green tomatoes and grapes. Pickling in vinegar is simply the safest, easiest, and most consistent way to get the most out of your food.

In the following recipes, you'll find some of my favorite pickling how-to's, some from my home kitchen and others from my restaurants. We'll also dive in to the relationship between vinegars and pickles, as well as some esoteric topics like the difference between lacto-fermented kosher-style pickles and vinegar pickles, which we explore in the kosher-style pickle recipe on page 59. But more on those topics later. Let's get pickling.

PICKLED CARROTS

Makes 1 quart

3 medium carrots, peeled, plus ¼ cup leafy carrot greens, stems removed

1 teaspoon red pepper flakes

1 dried bay leaf

1 cup rice vinegar (see variation, page 34)

1 cup water

1 cup kosher salt

½ cup sugar

3 tablespoons fish sauce

1 teaspoon carrot seeds (you can find at any good spice merchant or on Amazon)

1 teaspoon black peppercorns

One of my favorite sandwiches of all time is the Vietnamese bánh mì. When I lived in New York City, there was a great Vietnamese sandwich joint, Hanco's, not far from my apartment. I would go there whenever I had a day off and gorge myself. Everything about a bánh mì is great, but for me, what always stands out are the pickles, specifically the pickled carrots. We often overlook carrots as a star ingredient, so I took it upon myself to create a pickled carrot that would be a showstopper. Of course, these carrots work as the garnish to any sandwich, but I like them front and center in a salad, topped with fresh herbs and peanuts.

1 Using a mandoline, slice the carrots into ⅛-inch-thick planks. Run your knife lengthwise through the planks, cutting into matchsticks. Put the carrots, red pepper flakes, and bay leaf into a 1-quart mason jar.

2 In a saucepan over medium-high heat, combine the carrot greens, vinegar, water, salt, sugar, fish sauce, carrot seeds, and peppercorns and bring to a boil. Then, remove from the heat and let the pickling liquid cool a bit (it should still be warm).

3 Pour the pickling liquid over the carrots. Allow to cool to room temperature, put the lid on the jar, and transfer to the refrigerator for 48 hours to pickle. The pickle will keep, refrigerated, for up to 3 months.

PICKLED GREEN TOMATOES

Makes 1 quart

2 pounds overly ripe heirloom tomatoes

2½ tablespoons kosher salt

½ cup white wine vinegar (see variation, page 34)

3 garlic cloves, grated

1 tablespoon dried basil

2 pounds green, unripe cherry tomatoes

Living in Cleveland, you get used to a lot of things: snow, the Browns losing, and more snow, among other bummers. Combined, these things drive us Clevelanders to cherish our spring and summer. As soon as the winter weather breaks and the days are warmer than 50°F, we all start wearing shorts and T-shirts. As spring turns to summer, I have one thing on my mind: fresh tomatoes. I love tomatoes so much that at our restaurants we preserve as many as we can to carry a little slice of summer into the depths of winter. Pickled green tomatoes are always one of the things we make. We developed this recipe to showcase the one thing that pickled green tomatoes are often missing—tomato flavor.

1 Line a strainer or colander with three layers of cheesecloth.

2 Dice the heirloom tomatoes, place them in a large bowl with ½ tablespoon of the salt, and mix together gently with your hands.

3 Place the tomatoes in the prepared strainer. Carefully gather the corners of the cheesecloth and tie together tightly. Place the strainer into the bowl that held the tomatoes and leave uncovered in the refrigerator for 24 to 36 hours. Remove the strainer from the bowl; reserve both the tomato pulp and the tomato water separately.

4 Remove the tomato pulp from the cheesecloth, spread it on a baking sheet, and place in a 170°F oven for 2 hours, or dehydrate in a dehydrator at 125°F overnight.

Once dehydrated, grind the pulp in a spice grinder or a clean coffee grinder; it should be similar to flour in texture. Measure out 1 tablespoon for this recipe. Transfer the remainder to an airtight container and store in a cool, dry, dark place; it will keep indefinitely.

5 In a bowl, combine the vinegar, garlic, basil, tomato water, tomato powder, and remaining 2 tablespoons salt and stir to dissolve the salt.

6 Put the green cherry tomatoes into a 1-quart mason jar. Pour the liquid over them to cover. Place the lid on the jar and allow the tomatoes to ferment at room temperature for 5 to 7 days before using. The pickle will keep, refrigerated, indefinitely.

BAVARIAN BLACK GRAPE PICKLE

Makes 1 quart

1½ cups Old-School Red Wine Vinegar (page 34)

½ cup water

5 tablespoons sugar

1 tablespoon kosher salt

6 black peppercorns

3 allspice berries

1 whole star anise

1 fresh bay leaf

2 pounds table grapes, preferably black grapes or unripe green Concords, halved

Pretzels are a passion of mine, and my infatuation started when I was a kid. Every summer, my parents took me to Indians games at the old Cleveland Municipal Stadium, and they always gave me a small allowance to splurge on hot dogs, peanuts, or whatever else I wanted. The large soft pretzels stood out to me; we ate hot dogs and peanuts at home all the time but never soft pretzels. I'd get two, slather them with Cleveland's own Stadium Mustard, and watch the game. Later in life, as I evolved as a chef, I started to make my own pretzels. But a plain pretzel is a sad and lonely thing, so I've always whipped up a wide spread of mustards, cheeses, sausages, and pickles to serve alongside my precious twists. These pickled grapes are my favorite accompaniment.

1 In a medium saucepan, combine the vinegar, water, sugar, salt, peppercorns, allspice, star anise, and bay leaf and bring to a boil. Turn the heat to low and let simmer for 5 minutes. Remove the pickling liquid from the heat, strain it into a bowl, and discard the solids. Place the strained liquid, uncovered, in the refrigerator to cool completely.

2 In a 1-quart mason jar, combine the grapes and pickling liquid. Put the lid on the jar and transfer to the refrigerator for 4 days to pickle. The pickle will keep, refrigerated, for up to 4 months.

MODERN CLASSIC RED-ONION PICKLE

Makes 1 pint

1 cup water

½ cup Old-School Red Wine Vinegar (page 34)

½ cup kombucha

1 tablespoon kosher salt

1 tablespoon sugar

2 dried hibiscus flowers

1 large red onion, sliced

When it comes to classic vinegar pickles, you can't get more old-school than a red-onion pickle. This pickle can work in so many ways. From garnishing a Bloody Mary to a country pâté, this pickle has a place. Most recipes call for vinegar, salt, and sugar, but this recipe goes a step further and uses dried hibiscus flowers (you can find these at any spice merchant or Amazon) and vinegar's vinegary cousin kombucha. The kombucha adds a nice earthy sourness and probiotic spirit that takes this pickle to the next level. I like to use a nice fruity-flavored kombucha, one with strawberry, cherry, or other red fruit, to help this pickle shine even brighter.

1 In a small saucepan over high heat, combine the water, vinegar, kombucha, salt, sugar, and hibiscus flowers and bring to a simmer. As soon as the pickling liquid comes up to a simmer, turn off the heat.

2 Meanwhile, pack the onion into a 1-pint mason jar.

3 Once the pickling liquid simmers, remove it from the heat and carefully pour over the onion, being sure to completely cover the slices. Then transfer the jar, uncovered, to the refrigerator until cool to the touch, about 1 hour.

4 After the onion has cooled, put the lid on the jar and leave in the fridge for 24 hours to pickle. The pickle will keep, refrigerated, for up to 3 months.

WATERMELON RIND PICKLE

Makes 2 quarts

1 soccer ball–size
watermelon

2 quarts water

¾ cup rice vinegar
(see variation, page 34)

½ cup mirin

½ cup sugar

3 Thai bird chiles

2 fresh, frozen, or dried
lime leaves

1 whole star anise

1 cinnamon stick

8 coriander seeds

1 cup ice cubes

In 2011, Amelia and I had the opportunity to go to Japan. We had the best time and fell further in love with each other and with one of our favorite foods: ramen. Later that year, I was able to take my love of ramen to the next level and open my own Japanese-inspired noodle shop, Noodlecat. The opening chef, Brian Reilly, and I created some awesome food together, and to this very day this remains one of my favorite pickles of all time. Much love to Brian for this recipe.

1 Remove the white rind from the watermelon and cut it into 1-inch cubes; reserve the flesh for another use. Place the cubed melon rind into a large, airtight nonreactive container.

2 In a large pot over high heat, combine the water, vinegar, mirin, sugar, chiles, lime leaves, star anise, cinnamon, and coriander seeds. Bring to a boil and then immediately remove from the heat. Carefully pour the hot liquid over the watermelon rind, being sure to cover it completely.

3 Add the ice to the container and allow the liquid to cool to room temperature. Once it has cooled, cover and transfer to the refrigerator for 48 hours to pickle. The pickle will keep, refrigerated, for up to 6 months.

KOSHER-STYLE PICKLE
(AKA "IT'S NOT VINEGAR BUT THE pH IS THE SAME . . ." LACTIC ACID FERMENT)

Makes 1 quart

1 quart water

3 tablespoons pickling spice

2 tablespoons kosher salt

5 to 10 super-fresh Kirby pickling cucumbers (see Note)

1 bunch dill, with stems

1 dried red chile

2 fresh grape leaves, or 4 fresh oak leaves (grab them off the tree in your yard!)

2 small celery stalks from the center with the leaves attached, chopped into 2-inch-long pieces

1 medium onion, sliced thin

10 garlic cloves

There are two main types of pickles: ones made with vinegar and ones that are fermented. There are many chefs who argue over which one is better, but I don't feel that there's even an argument to be had—they're both kick-ass. When you really get down to it, the microbes that make vinegar and the ones that make fermented pickles are closely related, the main difference being that one produces acetic acid, aka vinegar, and the other produces lactic acid. The two acids taste so similar that even some pickle-makers can't tell the difference. This being so, you could argue that a vinegar pickle is just as fermented as a fermented one and vice versa. Here's an easy go-to kosher-style pickle that you can experiment with and tweak to your heart's desire.

The great thing about this recipe is that it can be easily changed to fit your taste preferences. If you want to swap out the cucumbers and spices listed for carrots and curry powder, then go for it. As long as your pickling liquid is made of 1 quart water and 2 tablespoons salt, you can improvise to infinity.

1 In a medium saucepan over high heat, combine the water, pickling spice, and salt. Let warm for 5 minutes, then stir to dissolve the salt. Once the salt is dissolved, remove from the heat and let the pickling liquid cool to room temperature.

2 While the pickling liquid cools, wash the cucumbers and shave off and discard a sliver from the blossom end (opposite the stem end); the blossom produces an enzyme that can cause your pickles to go soft. Cut off and finely chop the large stems of the dill. Set aside.

CONTINUED

3   Place the chile, grape leaves, celery, and chopped dill stems in the bottom of a 1-quart mason jar. Continue to layer in the cucumbers, onion slices, garlic, and dill fronds until they reach the shoulders of the jar, about ½ inch from the lip.

4   When the jar is filled, pour in the cooled pickling liquid so that all the veggies are submerged. Rest a dish or weight small enough to fit into the jar on top of the veggies; it needs to be heavy enough to keep them submerged. Wrap a coffee filter or piece of cheesecloth over the opening of the jar, secure it with a rubber band or butcher's twine, and leave out on your kitchen counter; at least 4 days for half-sour pickles or up to 9 days for sour pickles. After the pickles have reached the sourness you desire, cover the jar with the lid and transfer to the refrigerator. The pickle will keep, refrigerated, for up to 2 months.

NOTE Because the pickling cucumbers will be various sizes (small ones can be the size of a breakfast sausage; large ones can be as big around as a golf ball), you will need as many as will fit in the container.

GOODMAN'S GRILLED PICKLED ROMAINE LETTUCE

Makes 1 pint

1 cup water

¼ cup sugar

2 tablespoons Apple Cider Vinegar (page 35)

2 tablespoons Old-School Red Wine Vinegar (page 34)

2 tablespoons white wine vinegar (see variation, page 34)

2 tablespoons rice vinegar (see variation, page 34)

2 tablespoons sherry vinegar (see variation, page 34)

2 tablespoons honey

1 tablespoon maple syrup

1 teaspoon mustard seeds

1 cinnamon stick

1 sprig thyme

Freshly ground pepper

1 heart of romaine

Kosher salt

There are many times our local farmers grow such great foods that, after trying one bite, we buy them out. One year, the local lettuce was that deliciousness. After we bought all that we could, we realized that we could sell only so many salads. We decided that we had to look at romaine as more than just a salad or the garnish on a plate. Lettuce soup, lettuce ice cream, and this pickled lettuce recipe was born out of that experience, and we've been serving it at the Greenhouse Tavern ever since. I love using it to garnish the Greenhouse Tavern Veggie Burger (page 62) but also enjoy it as its own antipasto or even tossed with some fresh greens to make a killer pickled salad.

1 Preheat the grill to medium-high.

2 In a saucepan over medium heat, combine the water, sugar, all five vinegars, honey, maple syrup, mustard seeds, cinnamon, thyme, and 1 teaspoon pepper and bring to a simmer. Remove the pickling liquid from the heat and set aside.

3 Lightly season the romaine with salt and pepper and then grill for about 3 minutes on each side. Place the lettuce in a medium bowl.

4 Strain the still-warm pickling liquid, pour it over the grilled lettuce, and transfer the bowl to the refrigerator until cold. The pickle will keep, refrigerated, for up to 2 days.

 RETURN TO PAGE *61*

THE GREENHOUSE TAVERN VEGGIE BURGER

Makes 5 burgers

3 cups water

1 cup uncooked
long-grain brown rice

1 small turnip

1 small beet

1 small yellow onion

½ fennel bulb

2 garlic cloves

Kosher salt and freshly
ground pepper

1 cup cooked and
drained white beans,
pureed until smooth

2 tablespoons rice flour

2 tablespoons
grapeseed oil

5 brioche buns, toasted

Goodman's Grilled
Pickled Romaine Lettuce
(page 61) for serving

Mayonnaise (page 88)
for serving

As meat-centric as the Greenhouse Tavern is, I love me some veggies. When the Tavern opened, there were really only two veggie burgers available to us: the commercialized Morningstar option or a deep-fried portobello-mushroom cap. In the case of the latter (the current trendy option), the idea of using it as a burger just seemed uninspired and obvious. Instead, I created this veggie burger recipe, which is probably my fourth (if not tenth) attempt at perfecting it. We serve delicious fresh veggie juices at lunch every day and decided that, rather than throwing away the vegetable pulp or using it just in our stocks, we'd add it to our veggie-burger mix. The addition of beets or beet pulp gives the fully cooked meatless wonder the appearance of a medium-rare beef burger. It works perfectly for those days when my body needs a rejuvenating but satiating boost. The world needs more good veggie burgers like this one.

1 Preheat the oven to 350°F.

2 In a large saucepan over high heat, bring the water to a boil. Then, lower to a simmer, add the rice, and let simmer until fully cooked, about 40 minutes. Drain the rice, transfer to a baking sheet, and let cool.

3 In a food processor, combine the turnip, beet, onion, fennel, and garlic and pulse until the vegetables are finely minced and the same size as the rice grains. Place the minced vegetables on a baking sheet and season with salt and pepper. Roast the veggies until tender, about 20 minutes. Remove from the oven and let cool.

4 In a large bowl, gently mix the rice, roasted vegetables, and bean puree by hand. Once mixed, add the rice flour and mix again to incorporate. Still using your hands, shape the mixture into five 6-ounce patties.

5 In a large sauté pan over medium heat, warm the grapeseed oil. Add the patties and sear until golden brown in color, about 5 minutes per side.

6 Serve the patties on brioche buns with pickled lettuce and mayonnaise.

SAUERKRAUT

Makes 2 quarts

5 pounds red cabbage, cored and shredded

¼ cup kosher salt

½ cup Greenhouse Tavern–Style Craft-Beer Vinegar (page 32)

This is the ultimate pickle. No fuss, no frills—just great pickle flavor and tremendous crunch. Sauerkraut has a long history that stretches back to ancient China. It eventually made its way westward and was so beloved by Eastern and Northern Europeans that it became a backbone of their cuisines. In Cleveland, you'll find sauerkraut garnishing our beloved sauerkraut balls (see page 64), pierogi, and Polish boys. At my restaurant Trentina, we use copious amounts of sauerkraut, or *krauti* as the people of the northern Italian province of Trento say; we often comment that there's more sauerkraut than red sauce in the Alpine region. We prefer to use red cabbage for this, which produces a pickle that shines brighter than Dorothy's ruby reds. What makes this sauerkraut truly special is the infusion of beer vinegar at the end.

1 In a large bowl, using your hands, crush and squeeze the cabbage and salt together. Let sit, uncovered, at room temperature. After 30 minutes, you'll notice that the cabbage has "wept" a bit of water. Help this along by massaging and grinding the cabbage with your hands until you see about 2 cups of water in the bowl. You should be able to grab a handful of cabbage, squeeze it, and see a fair amount of liquid rain down into the bowl. This will be used as the pickling liquid.

2 Firmly pack the cabbage into two 1-quart mason jars until it reaches the shoulders of the jars, about ½ inch from the lip. Divide the pickling liquid that has accumulated in the bottom of the bowl evenly among both jars. Be sure to fill each jar with enough liquid to cover the cabbage. (If you need more liquid, use water.) Put the lids on the jars and let them sit at room temperature for 5 to 7 days. The longer sauerkraut sits, the more acidic it becomes.

3 After 5 to 7 days, carefully open the jars. (There will be some built-up pressure, so I recommend doing this in the sink just in case the jars spray.) Dump all the cabbage—now sauerkraut—and pickling liquid into a large bowl and add the vinegar. Mix everything well, then pack it back into the jars as before. Be sure to pour the pickling liquid back into the jars so that it covers the cabbage. Replace the lids and let the jars sit at room temperature for another 2 days before eating. The sauerkraut will keep, refrigerated, for up to 1 year.

 RETURN TO PAGE _63_

SAUERKRAUT BALLS

Makes 12 balls

2 tablespoons
unsalted butter

1 small yellow onion,
diced

4 garlic cloves, minced

1 cup minced speck (aka
smoked prosciutto)

3 tablespoons rye flour

1 cup drained
Sauerkraut (page 63)

1 tablespoon
Prosciutto-Scotch
Vinegar (page 37) or
white wine vinegar (see
variation, page 34)

1 tablespoon chopped
fresh dill

Kosher salt and freshly
ground pepper

1 quart rendered animal
fat, suet, or lard or
vegetable or canola oil

6 eggs

1 cup water

2 cups all-purpose flour

2 cups crushed panko
bread crumbs

Cocktail sauce, Dijon
Mustard (page 90),
and Mayonnaise
(page 88) for serving

I feel bad for those of you who have never visited or lived in northeastern Ohio, because that means you've most likely never enjoyed a leisurely game of euchre or had the awesomeness that is a sauerkraut ball. These awesome fritters hail from Akron, the home of King James. Go to any restaurant serving Eastern European food in the Cleveland/Akron area and you'll find these badass balls front and center. What wouldn't be great about a mix of sauerkraut and meat fried to a delicious golden crisp?

1   In a large sauté pan over medium heat, melt the butter. Add the onion and garlic and cook until translucent and aromatic, about 4 minutes. Add the speck and cook until it just starts to brown, about 2 minutes. Sprinkle the rye flour over everything and cook, stirring constantly, for an additional 3 minutes. Add the sauerkraut, vinegar, and dill. Cook until the liquid thickens, about 5 minutes. Taste and season with salt and pepper. Remove the pan from the heat and transfer the contents to a baking sheet or plate, spreading it into an even layer. Chill in the refrigerator, uncovered, for at least 2 hours or up to overnight.

2   When ready to cook, line a plate with paper towels. In a Dutch oven or other pot suitable for frying, heat the animal fat to 350°F on an instant-read thermometer. Crack the eggs into a narrow deep bowl, add the water, and whisk until thoroughly combined. Place the all-purpose flour into a shallow bowl and the crushed panko into another shallow bowl.

3   Remove the sauerkraut mixture from the refrigerator and roll into ping-pong-size balls. Roll a ball in the all-purpose flour to cover it completely; shake off any excess flour. Then, dip the ball into the egg mixture. Finally, completely coat the ball in the panko. Repeat with process for all the balls.

4   Using your hands, gently and carefully drop the balls, a few at a time, into the animal fat and fry until golden brown, about 4 minutes. Using a slotted spoon, remove from the fat and place on the prepared plate to drain.

5   Serve the balls hot with cocktail sauce, mustard, and mayo.

HOT & SPICY ROMANESCO GIARDINIERA

Makes 2 quarts

1 cup Old-School Red Wine Vinegar (page 34)

½ cup kosher salt

¼ cup sugar

4 teaspoons dried oregano

1 teaspoon red pepper flakes

1 teaspoon mustard seeds

1 teaspoon carrot seeds (you can find at any good spice merchant or on Amazon) or caraway seeds

1 teaspoon chili powder

1 teaspoon crushed black peppercorns

3 boquerones (you can find in any Italian market)

1 head romanesco, cut into small florets

2 carrots, sliced into ⅛-inch-thick coins

1 salsify, peeled and cut into ⅛-inch-thick coins

1 red bell pepper, cut into ¼-inch strips and seeds removed

2 celery stalks, sliced

3 Fresno chiles, thinly sliced, with seeds

3 garlic cloves, peeled and smashed

½ cup "silver standard" olive oil (see page 23)

1 tablespoon minced fresh oregano

If you were to come to my house and open my refrigerator, you would see no fewer than twelve different types of pickles. I love them all: spicy, half-sour, Asian, Italian—you name it, I typically have it. Giardiniera, the classic Italian pickled veggie mix that is a staple of Midwestern sub shops, is always present, for the reason that it combines several of my favorite pickles into one delicious mix. This recipe takes a traditional giardiniera and amps it up with carrot seeds, *boquerones* (Spanish pickled white anchovies), salsify, and romanesco.

1 In a small saucepan over medium heat, combine vinegar, salt, sugar, dried oregano, red pepper flakes, mustard seeds, carrot seeds, chili powder, peppercorns, and boquerones. Bring the pickling liquid to a simmer and then turn off the heat.

2 In a large bowl, combine the romanesco, carrots, salsify, bell pepper, celery, chiles, and garlic and stir to mix.

3 Pack the mixture into two 1-quart mason jars until it reaches the shoulders of the jars, about ½ inch from the lip. Pour the pickling liquid over the vegetables, being sure to cover the vegetables completely. Put the lids on the jars and transfer to the refrigerator.

4 After 3 days, in a small bowl, mix together the olive oil and fresh oregano. Open the jars, pour half of the herbed oil into each, and then replace the lids. The giardiniera is now ready to eat and will keep, refrigerated, indefinitely.

MUFFULETTA SANDO

Serves 4

OLIVE SALAD

1 red bell pepper

1 cup mixed pitted olives

1 cup Hot & Spicy Romanesco Giardiniera (page 67)

4 fresh basil leaves, torn

¼ cup torn fresh parsley leaves

2 teaspoon white wine vinegar (see variation, page 34), plus more as needed

1 tablespoon "silver standard" olive oil (see page 23), plus more as needed

1 muffuletta loaf or 10-inch round focaccia

¼ pound sliced speck (aka smoked prosciutto)

¼ pound sliced finocchiona salami

¼ pound sliced capocollo ham

¼ pound sliced mortadella

¼ pound sliced provolone piccante

New Orleans is an interesting place that has long captivated me. It's a city of dichotomy: on one hand, it was the longest-operating port for the slave trade in America; on the other, it's one of the most diverse and unique cultures in the country. I've spent many vacations in New Orleans and have eaten more than my fair share of food there, but the one item that I enjoy the most is the muffuletta sandwich, because it's the perfect pairing of ingredients between sliced bread. So I always have a plethora of pickles, cured meats, and cheeses in my house, which allows me to enjoy this sandwich whenever I want.

1 To make the olive salad: Turn one of the stove-top burners to high (this will work for either a gas or electric stove). Using tongs, roast the bell pepper directly in the flame (or on the coil, if using an electric stove top), turning occasionally, until the skin is black and blistered, about 4 minutes per side. Place the pepper in a bowl, cover tightly with plastic wrap, and let sit for 20 minutes. Then, remove the plastic wrap and, using your fingers, rub the charred skin off the pepper. Remove and discard the stem and seeds, chop the pepper into small dice, and place it back in the bowl.

2 On a cutting board, combine and coarsely chop the olives and giardiniera. Add them to the bowl with the bell pepper. Add the basil, parsley, vinegar, and olive oil to the bowl and mix together. Taste and add more vinegar and oil as needed. Cover and refrigerate for up to 2 weeks.

3 Horizontally slice the muffuletta loaf in half through the equator. Spread all of the olive salad on each half of the loaf.

4 Layer the meats and cheeses on one half of the loaf and then top with the other half to close the sandwich. Wrap the sandwich in parchment paper and let sit for 20 minutes at room temperature, so the olive salad soaks into the bread. Slice into wedges and serve.

KIMCHI

Makes 3 quarts

¼ cup kosher salt

2 tablespoons mochi sweet rice flour

2 tablespoons Korean chile flakes

½ cup Greenhouse Tavern–Style Craft-Beer Vinegar (page 32)

½ cup water

1 bunch scallions, white and tender green parts, sliced on the diagonal

1 pound daikon radish

1 apple (preferably GoldRush or Arkansas Black)

1 medium white onion

4 garlic cloves

1 large head napa cabbage

Kimchi is the gateway drug that leads you down the spiral into the world of fermentation. The salty-and-sour taste, spicy flavor, and crispy crunch always leave me craving more. This is the kimchi that we've been making at Noodlecat since it opened.

1 In a large bowl, combine the salt, rice flour, and chile flakes. Whisk in the vinegar and water, then the scallions, and set aside. Using a box grater, shred the daikon, apple, onion, and garlic into the seasoned vinegar and stir to combine.

2 Using a mandoline or a knife, cut the cabbage into thin strips. Add the cabbage to the bowl with the other ingredients. Using your hands, squeeze and mix everything together for 5 minutes.

3 Evenly divide and pack the mixture into three 1-quart mason jars. Put the lids on the jars and leave at room temperature for 3 days to ferment and pickle. After 3 days, it is ready to eat. The kimchi will keep, refrigerated, indefinitely.

FERMENTED HOT SAUCE

Makes about 1 quart

2 pounds fresh
Fresno chiles

2 chipotle chiles

1½ tablespoons
kosher salt

1 tablespoon ground
mustard seeds

2 cups Apple Wine
Vinegar (page 36)

There's a phrase often heard in professional kitchens: *Put an egg on it*. When chefs and cooks use this phrase, it means to take a dish to the next level. Be it with caviar or 10 grams of white truffle, most dishes can be elevated in a soigné manner. In my kitchen, this hot sauce is my egg; when I put this on something, it goes from drab to fab. Its versatility is astonishing, enhancing everything from scrambled eggs (why put an egg on it when you can put it on an egg) to chicken stock. Go ahead and put some freakin' sauce on it. Like Beyoncé, I always keep a bottle of hot sauce in my purse.

Although we prefer fresh Fresno chiles for this sauce, you can really use any chile you like. It's always a good idea to wear gloves or wash your hands often with hot soapy water when working with all chiles. Imagine the burn in your mouth hitting your skin or eyes.

1   In a food processor, combine the Fresno and chipotle chiles, salt, and mustard seeds and process until a paste forms, about 2 minutes. Transfer the paste to a 1-quart mason jar and seal the lid. Allow to sit at room temperature for 5 days.

2   After 5 days, open the jar and put the paste back into the food processor. Turn on the processor and slowly stream in the vinegar and process until a smooth sauce forms. Strain the sauce through a fine-mesh sieve back into the mason jar. (Save the solids that you strain out, then dehydrate them and crush to make hot chili powder; refer to the tomato powder instructions on page 52. It tastes great on chocolate ice cream.) The hot sauce will keep, refrigerated, for up to 12 months.

Trentina

3 COLD VINEGAR-BASED SAUCES

(AKA VINAIGRETTES)

Here's some real talk: Vinaigrettes are the gateway drug to cooking with vinegars. Awakening your taste buds, they help you pick up flavors your tongue might otherwise miss.

Vinaigrettes aren't just a condiment to throw onto your sorry shredded-carrot-and-iceberg-lettuce salads. Within the vinegar world, vinaigrettes are like the little black dress or your favorite leather jacket. You can put them on simple steamed broccoli, poached fish, or Cuban-style pork chops and they'll make all three things taste, well, better. They're incredibly versatile. While vinaigrettes can be either made hot (in the pan, if you will) or cold, we'll focus specifically on the chillier recipes in this section to introduce you to the world of sour. (We'll touch on hot vinegar-based sauces, aka pan sauces, in chapter 5.)

To start, let's talk about what cold vinaigrettes (better known in the food world as cold vinegar-based sauces) are: a combo of liquids (usually oil and vinegar) and seasonings. When created in the right ratio and with the right balance, they create a riot of flavors that work as building blocks in your kitchen arsenal.

Cold vinaigrettes have their first historical mentions in antiquity, but they certainly appeared long before that. Determining when we first started using them is "nearly impossible," as Alan Davidson points out in *The Oxford Companion to Food*. Trying to pin down the who, where, and when of these sauces' first use is much like trying to figure out who first domesticated fire. They are that fundamental to modern cooking.

What we can imagine happening with the first vinaigrette is perhaps the same thing that occurred with alcohol; some ancient idiot savant probably left alcohol out and exposed it to air, which eventually turned it to vinegar. Because vinegar by itself is typically too harsh and pungent to eat alone, the inadvertent inventor of cold vinegar-based sauces needed something to tame its bite. Maybe at some point that individual was eating a fatty cut of meat (fats are great at coating our mouths and taming intense tastes) and happened to take a sip of the converted alcohol. The result probably caused fireworks to go off on his tongue, leading to the classic pairing of acid and fat.

Eventually, cold vinegar-based sauces saw their functionality evolve. Fundamental food preservation (in the days before refrigeration) relied heavily on both salt and vinegar. Foods preserved in this method also needed to be placed in containers that didn't allow air to come into contact with the food. If air penetrated the containers, the food would spoil. If people couldn't find the appropriate vessel, they'd pour oils and other rendered animal fats on top of the mixture to create a barrier between the brine and the surrounding air. The result? Items preserved in this way created what we today call *broken vinaigrettes*, in which the oil and vinegar separate. These early vinegar-makers then took their experimentation one step further by discovering that these cold vinegar-based sauces could also be made by holding their liquids in suspension—birthing what we call *emulsified vinaigrettes*. No matter if the sauce is cold or hot, broken or emulsified, our vinegar-making forefathers found that the optimum flavor-magnifying ratio is 3:1 oil to vinegar. People then caught on to the glory of these sauces and— eureka!—devised methods to create these sauces on their own.

Historical texts dating from the time of the ancient Romans, around 100 BCE, make mention of wild greens being seasoned with salt, olive oil, and vinegar. If we fast-forward approximately 1,500 years, we see many mentions of cold vinegar-based sauces starting to appear in texts—like Platina's ruminations on seasoned lettuce in a 1475 publication titled *On Right Pleasure and Good Health*. It's around this time that we also start to notice cold vinegar-based sauces evolve in other ways. Besides aiding food preservation, cold vinegar-based sauces were thought to have medicinal and therapeutic qualities. However, some enterprising vinegar-makers discovered these sauces were also just flat-out enjoyable to consume. As education levels rose and societies transitioned from feudalism to capitalism, the access to and new uses of vinegar and cold vinegar-based sauces became more common. People of all social and economic classes could now afford these ingredients, as opposed to just wealthy individuals as before.

The first modern writings that concerned cold vinegar-based sauces come courtesy of "the glutton of gluttons," Jean Anthelme Brillat-Savarin. Brillat-Savarin published an epic tome on gastronomy called *The Physiology of Taste* in 1825. In it, he tells the tale of a French aristocrat and culinary savant named d'Albignac who lived in London. Here's how it unfolds: d'Albignac was chillin' in a tavern when some young posh dudes approached him. Knowing that d'Albignac was French (at the time, the French were known as excellent salad-tossers), they asked him to toss their salad (literally—get your mind out of the gutter). He obliged, and the salad was so mind-blowing that they recommended d'Albignac to all of their friends. Before long, d'Albignac was running London's salad-tossing game, hitting up rich people's houses to flex his skills and working out of a custom-made kit of the finest mahogany. When d'Albignac eventually made enough money off the rich, he created replica versions of his salad-tossing kits, stocking them with one hundred different oils, vinegars, herbs, and spices. Without knowing it, this vinaigrette hustler invented bottled salad dressing.

Soon after d'Albignac sold his mahogany-enclosed salad dressings, canning technology stepped up its game. Fellow Frenchman Nicolas Appert pioneered a vessel that brought cold vinegar-based sauces to the masses in less expensive tin and/or glass bottles.

But it wasn't until Henry J. Heinz flipped our collective lid that we got to know cold vinegar-based sauces as they appear today. Case in point: ketchup. Heinz's company, with the help of the company's main food scientist, G. F. Mason, revolutionized our understanding of food safety and allowed Heinz to package and sell his dressings in mass quantities.

He and Mason also innovated a way to preserve their iconic condiments without using toxic preservatives (nineteenth-century producers shadily used gross crap like chalk, lead, and formaldehyde to preserve tomato-based condiments), and Heinz, based on his business's transparency-first model, pioneered the use of clear, glass bottles to show his consumers what they were buying.

Nowadays, every one of our homes has a bottle of ketchup, mustard, or dressing that showcases vinegar's dominating presence, even if it isn't your pantry's showstopper. Let's start with my favorite condiment recipe to show how versatile vinegar really is.

HOUSE KETCHUP

Makes about 1 quart

1 tablespoon
sunflower oil

½ pound yellow onions,
finely diced

Kosher salt

1½ teaspoons
smoked paprika

1 teaspoon
sweet paprika

1 teaspoon black
peppercorns

½ teaspoon freshly
cracked cloves

½ teaspoon cracked
allspice berries

½ teaspoon
mustard powder

1 fresh or dried bay leaf

1 tablespoon peeled and
grated, fresh ginger

2 tablespoons dark
brown sugar

4 garlic cloves, peeled
and smashed

1 tablespoon
tomato paste

2 cups fresh, peeled,
or canned tomatoes
(with no additional
ingredients)

1 tablespoon Sriracha

½ cup Apple Cider
Vinegar (page 35)

2 tablespoons
distilled vinegar

Ketchup, which in its original form was *ke-tchup*, literally translates to "fish sauce" in an older dialect of Polynesian. Nowadays, *ke-tchup*'s modern form, tomato-based ketchup, is the most widely available condiment around the world.

Ke-tchup came to the West about 1690 via the imperial trading companies of the British Isles, who treasured it when it came over from Southeast Asia. It was their version of gold watches. If you were serving it, you were the real deal. You weren't aristocracy if you didn't harvest salt from Vienna, peppercorns from China, and/or fish sauce from Southeast Asia.

We can thank the British for informing us about the unpleasant realities of sea scurvy, the product behind the wonderful initialism IPA, and the word *posh* ("Port Out, Starboard Home"), and we can also salute some crafty Englishman who couldn't afford that fancy *ke-tchup* for inventing what we now know as ketchup. The spiced ketchup from the British Isles was made of various items because of cost, necessity, and preference; walnuts and mushrooms were used in the first documented English-procured ketchups, but eventually tomatoes made their way into the mix. Once American industrialists took a liking to the sauce, perfecting its canning and preservation, ketchup became the beloved condiment that it is today.

Making our house ketchup is as easy as making a casserole or whipping up apple butter (which isn't even butter, but don't get me started on that). For this recipe, you'll want to use a slow cooker. Granted, you can make a great ketchup by cooking it in a pot on the stove top, but the way to get a transformative house ketchup is to use a slow cooker.

1   In a slow cooker, combine the sunflower oil and onions and season heavily with salt. Cover and cook, stirring occasionally, for 30 minutes over low heat or for 15 minutes over high heat. Don't caramelize your onions; just extract the natural sugars. Add water, a tablespoon at a time, if parts of your onions look like they are coloring. The slow cooker should remain covered during most of the cooking process. Only remove the lid to stir the ingredients when needed.

2   Stir both paprikas, the pepper-corns, cloves, allspice, mustard powder, bay leaf, and ginger into the onions and cook for 2 minutes over high heat, stirring until the mixture is aromatic. Add the brown sugar, garlic, and tomato paste and use a wooden spoon to mash and stir them vigorously for 1 minute until everything is combined homogeneously.

3   Now, add the tomatoes, then add the Sriracha and both vinegars, and season with salt. Deglaze the slow cooker by scraping up bits of food stuck to the bottom. (Heads up: If you add Sriracha or vinegar to a hot slow cooker, your sinuses will clear.) Simmer, partially covered, until the ketchup is thick, 1½ hours over high heat or 5 to 9 hours over low heat.

4   Using a ladle, transfer the hot ketchup to a blender and puree it, making sure to follow the blender instructions for safety (over high speed in small batches, as hot ingredients blend finer than cold). Transfer to an airtight, nonreactive vessel, like a 1-quart mason jar. The ketchup will keep, refrigerated, for up to 3 months.

NOODLECAT'S POWER KETCHUP

Makes about 1 quart

3 cups House Ketchup (page 78) or your favorite bottled variety

1 tablespoon rice vinegar (see variation, page 34)

2 tablespoons tamari

2 tablespoons sambal oelek

2 teaspoons peeled and grated fresh ginger

1 small jalapeño chile

1 scallion, white and tender green parts, sliced

1 garlic clove, grated

Zest and juice of 1 lime

This is a gnarly and nasty cousin to American ketchup. It echoes how we think about our Noodlecat restaurant—Japanese sensibilities through the American lens—so having an amped-up ketchup with ginger, scallion, and tamari is a natural complement to regular ketchup. What started as an attempt to Japan-ify America's most famous condiment became our catchall for steamed buns, wing sauces, and dressed-up, crispy brussels sprouts. Essentially, it tasted so delicious that we used it on everything and gave it a lifetime place on Noodlecat's menu. Now I want to give you the power to do the same with this utility-player condiment.

In a food processor, combine the ketchup, vinegar, tamari, sambal oelek, ginger, jalapeño, scallion, garlic, lemon zest, and lemon juice and blend until smooth. (Keep in mind that it won't look Heinz-smooth, but it will be smooth enough.) Transfer to an airtight, nonreactive 1-quart container. The ketchup will keep, refrigerated, for up to 4 months.

 RETURN TO PAGE *78 or 80*

THE GREENHOUSE TAVERN'S PROPER POMMES FRITES

Serves 2

2 large Idaho russet potatoes

½ gallon fry oil

Kosher salt

House Ketchup (page 78) or Noodlecat's Power Ketchup (facing page) for serving

Our pommes frites are an example of a mundane recipe that's completely transformed by proper sourcing and cooking technique. Believe it or not, making the perfect fry, with a salty crunchy exterior and a pillowy interior, requires a three-day process. On the first day, we select older starchier potatoes, cut them into batons (stick shapes), and soak and rinse out any extra starch. On the second day, we blanch in oil and dry them out, forming a pellicle (a dried exterior); this day's work is crucial. Think about a Five Guys or In-N-Out french fry. Yeah, they serve french fries, but they simply cut and deep-fry their product, not allowing enough time for the crucial exoskeleton to develop. By the third day of our process, we've achieved that structural perfection and can finally deep-fry the perfect pommes frites.

I specifically mention using old Idaho russet potatoes for pommes frites because potatoes that have been cellared (stored) and aged after harvest have more starch in them than sugar. Freshly dug potatoes have a higher sugar content and are therefore more prone to burning during cooking, especially frying. So use a starchy potato that has less of a chance of burning. We also encourage using Idaho russets because they're flavorful and cook up incredibly well. Please keep in mind that the oil you use for frying is important; if possible, purchase already rendered animal fat (preferably cow, chicken, or duck) from a butcher or grocer. We love beef fat at Greenhouse Tavern.

1 Cut the potatoes into ¼-inch-thick rectangular batons and immediately submerge them in a large bowl of water to cover for at least 1 hour or up to 24 hours, depending on your level of commitment (the longer the soak, the better the fry).

2 Pour the fry oil into a deep pot; leave enough room so the oil won't spill over when the potatoes are added. Heat the oil to 275°F on an instant-read thermometer.

3 Line two baking sheets with a double thickness of paper towel.

4 Drain the potatoes into a colander, rinse under cold water until the water runs clear, and then dry them thoroughly. Add the potatoes to the oil and blanch them for 6 minutes, then transfer to one of the prepared baking sheets to drain.

CONTINUED

5 Generously season the fries with salt, and let them rest uncovered in the refrigerator overnight. This forms a pellicle of outer flesh on the fry, yielding it more crispy than soggy. Leave the oil in the pot, cover with a lid, and reserve.

6 The next day, reheat the oil to 350°F on an instant-read thermometer.

7 Add the fries in batches, cold and straight from the refrigerator, to the oil, not overcrowding the pot, and cook until they achieve a crispy golden outside and airy potato center, 5 to 6 minutes. (To know if you've got the airy center, eat one in order to test it.) Season with salt. Serve immediately with ketchup.

VARIATION Oven fries are almost as good. Just cut and soak the potatoes as directed, then toss in 2 tablespoons "bronze standard" olive oil (see page 23). Spread out the pommes frites, with ample space for crisping, on a parchment paper–lined baking sheet and bake in a 375°F oven for 25 minutes.

AIOLI

Makes about 1¹/₂ cups

10 garlic cloves

1 teaspoon kosher salt

1 egg yolk

1 cup "gold standard" olive oil (see page 23)

This is a traditional Galician aioli that's the perfect staple condiment for any garlic lover. To keep with the spirit of the condiment's Spanish origins, we use a mortar and pestle to complete this entire recipe. Once finished, use it over fried potatoes to make *patatas bravas*, Spanish white potatoes that have been fried in oil and served with a sauce (i.e., your aioli).

For this recipe, the hotter and spicier the raw garlic you use, the better; try either Bogatyr or Spanish Roja garlic if you can find it. These are two of my favorite varieties of garlic that my friend Fred Thaxton grows on his farm. If you don't have a personal hookup, you should be able to find both of these garlic types at your local farmers' market.

With a chilled mortar and pestle, pulverize the garlic and salt to a fine paste. Add the egg yolk to the mortar and continue to thoroughly mix everything together with the pestle. Carefully add the olive oil, drop by drop, making sure to forcefully stir the garlic mixture to make an emulsion. Continue to mix until the oil is completely used and the mixture is emulsified and totally opaque, 10 to 15 minutes. Transfer to an airtight, nonreactive 1-quart container and cover. The aioli will keep, refrigerated, for up to 3 days.

 RETURN TO PAGE *84*

PICKLES & EGG SALAD SANDWICH

Serves 3

1 tablespoon salted cultured butter

6 Pullman loaf slices (white, wheat, seeded, etc.), about ¾ inch thick

4 hard-cooked eggs

½ cup Aioli (facing page)

½ cup fines herbes (see page 232)

¼ cup diced firm fermented pickle (see page 59), with some juice

1 tablespoon drained and diced capers

1 tablespoon Dijon mustard (see page 90)

1 teaspoon chili powder

Zest and juice of 1 lemon

4 to 6 thin slices each cucumber, celery, in-season tomatoes, and red onion (or any fresh vegetable that's popping in your local farmers' market or garden)

¼ cup sprouted chickpeas or lentils, or other sprouts

Kosher salt and freshly ground pepper

I'll be honest, I don't love toasters. When it comes to making toast, I prefer a large, buttered cast-iron skillet on the stove top, in the oven, or under the broiler. You'll want to use this tool to reach toast nirvana. Once you've secured your mighty skillet, you can make this dish several different ways: à la toast with tarragon, tomato, and sprouted seeds; with blanched asparagus; with boiled rose veal tongue; or with anything, really, as long as it's on toast.

However, my one steadfast rule that you must follow for this recipe is to find a "sandwich buddy." In all our restaurant kitchens, the sandwich buddy functions as a bonding mate with whom you'll share your (I'm assuming) ingenious creation. He or she now owes you one half of a sandwich upon its creation, and you to his or her next sammy. It's ideal to regularly swap with your buddy, but, like all casual relationships, this partnership doesn't have to be monogamous. It's more of an olive branch to show acceptance to a newbie or recent recipient of a lacing.

This sandwich is filled with a mayonnaise-based mixture known at fancier restaurants as sauce gribiche, which dates back over a hundred years to Escoffier. A young kosher pickle or cornichon will work well in the gribiche, or you Chicago homers can substitute that famous, mildly poisonous, neon pickle relish. I also highly recommend using our mayonnaise recipe in this sandwich filling; however, if you'd prefer a store-bought version, you'll be best served with one of these three brands: Sir Kensington's, Duke's, or Maille.

1   Spread the butter on both sides of the bread slices.

2   In a cast-iron skillet over medium-high heat, quickly toast each side of each slice to achieve color and texture, without drying out the bread, up to 5 minutes. If you toast it too long and slow, it turns into bread crumbs.

3   Peel the hard-cooked eggs and cut them in half. Very finely chop the yolks and cut the whites into a small dice.

4   In a medium bowl, combine the chopped egg yolks, diced egg whites, aioli, fines herbes, pickle and its juice, capers, mustard, chili powder, lemon zest, and lemon juice. Mix well to form a sauce gribiche.

CONTINUED

PICKLES & EGG SALAD SANDWICH, CONTINUED

5   Spread the gribiche on one side of each piece of toast from edge to edge, making sure to maintain an even, thin coating. Add even layers of cucumber, celery, tomato, and onion and the sprouts; seasoning each item with salt and pepper to provide your sandwich with an overall flavor as opposed to pointed concentrations of taste. Top the veggies with the remaining toasts, gribiche-sides down. Using a sharp serrated knife, cut the sandwiches from corner to corner, forming two triangles from each. Serve immediately.

VARIATION Incorporate 1 tablespoon crème fraîche and ¼ cup diced radish into the sauce gribiche to kick the whole recipe up a notch.

MAYONNAISE

Makes about 1 cup

2 egg yolks

1 tablespoon
Greenhouse Tavern–
Style Craft-Beer Vinegar
(page 32)

1 teaspoon
mustard powder

1 teaspoon high-quality
natural salt (such as
Redmond Real Salt;
don't use anything
iodized)

1 cup high-quality
neutral oil or "gold
standard" olive oil
(see page 23)

1 tablespoon cold water

1 tablespoon seasoning
of your choice (optional;
see headnote

After my mother's long and stressful labor, my father was holding newborn Jonathon Sawyer, while eating a ham sandwich, and a mayonnaise-laden drop landed on my forehead, thus anointing my still-forming brain with an affection not only for cooking but also for mayo. In my home fridge, I typically have three mayonnaises: a house-made, an aioli-style mayonnaise, and Duke's. Here, I cover an everyday mayo.

For this recipe, you'll need to utilize the "gold standard" emulsification method (see page 90). If money is of no consequence, use a "gold standard" olive oil, but dispense it from a squeeze bottle or pour-spouted measuring cup to control the flow. You may also like adding a seasoning to this mayonnaise— your choice. If I want to get fancy, I prefer mayo with curry paste, but garlic puree and/or jerk rub are acceptable derivations. Incorporating the seasoning as you're making the initial recipe allows for a more complete infusion; however, it's not paramount and you can gently stir in the seasoning after you finish the recipe.

1   Fill a large bowl with ice and rest a smaller bowl in it.

2   In the smaller bowl, combine the egg yolks, vinegar, mustard powder, and salt and whisk together. Add the oil, drop by drop, while vigorously whisking; these two things are key. Once the mixture begins to change color and ribbon (meaning the mixture forms ribbon-shaped streaks as you move the whisk back and forth), increase the increment of oil from mere drops to a small, steady stream. Whisk in the cold water once half of the oil has been incorporated, 3 to 5 minutes.

3   If desired, stir the seasoning into the mayonnaise, then pour the finished mixture into an airtight container and cover. The mayonnaise will keep, refrigerated, for up to 1 week.

CLASSIC ENGLISH PEA & ONION SALAD

Serves 4

5 ounces bacon, cut into ¼-inch cubes

2 eggs

3 tablespoons Mayonnaise (facing page)

2 tablespoons Apple Wine Vinegar (page 36)

1 tablespoon "silver standard" olive oil (see page 23)

1 small yellow onion, chopped

¼ cup grated Parmesan cheese

¼ cup chopped fresh soft herbs, such as tarragon, parsley, mint, and basil

Zest and juice of 1 lemon

Kosher salt and freshly ground pepper

2 cups shelled fresh or frozen English peas

2 tablespoons chopped Marcona almonds

2 tablespoons bread crumbs (see page 27)

Think of this salad as a little nostalgic slice of the preparation of canned and frozen products of the mid-twentieth century. I've had versions made with Miracle Whip; cubed deli cheese; ranch dressing powder; French's Crispy Fried Onions; spice additions of curry, Sriracha, and Dijon mustard; and even broccoli in place of the peas. However, I love using organic frozen or shelled fresh peas—just not canned ones. The real beauty of having a salad like this on the holiday table is that it's a delicious tart yet sweet break from the overindulgence of roasted birds, velvety gravy, and buttery potatoes.

1 Preheat the oven to 400°F. Line a plate with paper towels.

2 Place the bacon in an even layer on a baking sheet and bake until it's fully cooked and crispy, about 15 minutes. Strain off the rendered fat, transfer the bacon to the prepared plate to absorb excess grease, and let cool. (Save the rendered fat for other cooking adventures.) Set aside.

3 Place the eggs in a small saucepan, cover them with water, and bring to a boil. Turn off the heat and let the eggs sit for 10 minutes. Then, drain and run the eggs under cold water for 10 minutes to cool them down. Once the eggs are cool, peel and chop them.

4 In a small bowl, combine the mayonnaise, vinegar, olive oil, onion, ⅛ cup of the Parmesan, ⅛ cup of the herbs, the lemon zest, lemon juice, and chopped eggs. Season the dressing with salt and pepper.

5 If using fresh peas, coarsely chop them to tenderize; if using frozen peas, defrost them under cold running water and drain off the excess moisture. Add the peas to the dressing and gently mix together. Transfer to an appropriate serving vessel. Evenly layer the remaining ⅛ cup herbs, remaining ⅛ cup Parmesan, the almonds, bread crumbs, and, finally, the bacon on top of the salad. Serve immediately.

VARIATION If you want to personalize the recipe, when you add the chopped eggs to the dressing, also add curry powder, aged Montgomery Cheddar, Old Bay Seasoning, ranch seasoning, Sriracha, or sautéed morels. I've yet to find something that doesn't work in this salad. Go crazy!

DIJON MUSTARD

Makes about 2 cups

2 cups mustard seeds

½ cup good white wine (preferably a Burgundy Chardonnay), chilled

¼ cup ice-cold water

¼ cup distilled vinegar or sharp white wine vinegar (see variation, page 34)

2 teaspoons kosher salt

Mustard is a food that I feel that we take for granted. We're accustomed to several different kinds of prepackaged, mass-produced varieties that, while they have their uses, don't represent the condiment's pinnacle. Few people actually make their mustard at home nowadays. This recipe is not only a game changer, which you'll want to slather on everything from hot dogs to salads, but is so simple that you can memorize it after your first attempt. White Burgundy (*Bourgogne*) is the ultimate French Chardonnay, and can be found from four different production areas within the Burgundy region.

1 With a mortar and pestle, crush the mustard seeds; making sure you *don't* pulverize into a fine powder.

2 In a medium bowl, combine the wine, water, vinegar, and crushed seeds and stir to mix. Transfer to the refrigerator and let rest for at least 24 hours or up to 72 hours (the longer it sits, the hotter and more pungent it will become).

3 When ready, transfer the mixture to a food processor, add the salt, and puree for 90 seconds to combine.

4 Place the mixture in an airtight, nonreactive 1-pint container, cover, and let sit at room temperature out of direct sunlight for 3 days; it will then be ready to use. The mustard will keep, refrigerated, indefinitely.

DIJON VINAIGRETTE

Makes 1 quart

2 tablespoons
mustard seeds

1 cup Dijon Mustard
(facing page) or store-
bought spicy Dijon
mustard, preferably
Maille

1 cup Greenhouse
Tavern–Style Craft-Beer
Vinegar (page 32), or
English malt vinegar

Zest and juice of
½ lemon

½ cup "silver standard"
olive oil (see page 23) or
blended oil (see page 22)

Kosher salt

Here's how hip-hop legend Nas inadvertently breaks down the vinaigrette-making process: Oil and water don't mix. Unless we're emulsifying them chemically and physically. When it comes to standard vinaigrette, you've got two kinds: broken (the oil and vinegar are separated) and emulsified, which I'll focus on now. The process of emulsification in vinaigrettes is achieved by starting with an acid, sometimes a mustardy or eggy one, and slowly blending in oil. Looking at your local grocery store's salad dressings, you'll encounter broken vinaigrettes like Italian, where the oil and water are clearly separated, and emulsified vinaigrettes like Caesar dressing, mayonnaise, and the ubiquitous brown balsamic (your Wishbone, Kraft, Newman's Own are all emulsified in the bottle), where everything has come together.

1 In a small bowl, combine the mustard seeds and 1 cup water and let soak for 24 hours, then drain.

2 Using your chosen method (see box), combine the mustard, vinegar, lemon zest, and lemon juice and blend. Slowly add the olive oil, drop by drop, until it's emulsified (i.e., when the oil and water become opaque), no more than 2 minutes. Keep it cold and don't overblend, which will bitter your vinaigrette.

3 Season with salt and then fold in the mustard seeds. Transfer to an airtight container. The vinaigrette will keep, refrigerated, for up to 1 year.

Based on the equipment you have in your kitchen and your own level of commitment to making emulsified vinegar-based sauces, these are the best courses of action to create this recipe.

BEST RESULTS (GOLD STANDARD) Whisking by hand is the most laborious method; chill your bowl and whisk for best results.

SECOND-BEST RESULTS (SILVER STANDARD) Use a chilled stick blender; submerge the blending end in ice water for 20 minutes prior.

THIRD-BEST RESULTS (BRONZE STANDARD) Use a blender; you may need to double or triple the recipe so that the base ingredients reach the blades.

FOURTH-BEST RESULTS ("PARTICIPATION MEDAL" STANDARD) Use a food processor.

 RETURN TO PAGE 91

RED WINE–BRAISED LENTILS & FRISÉE SALAD DIJON

Serves 2

1 cup French green lentils

1 cup Old-School Red Wine Vinegar (page 34)

1 cup red wine

1 cup stock mirepoix (see page 24)

Kosher salt and freshly ground pepper

1 cup diced salad mirepoix (see page 24)

2 tablespoons minced parsley

¼ to ½ cup Dijon Vinaigrette (page 91)

1 head frisée lettuce or chicory, extremely coarse-chopped

2 tablespoons grated bottarga

¼ cup bread crumbs (see page 27)

2 poached eggs (optional)

¼ cup diced crispy cooked bacon (optional)

I had an epiphany one day where I was able to take a classical French dish and elevate it. However, let me give you some background on the salad first. It can trace its origins to southern France, where it's typically served as a light midday meal. Traditionally, chefs prepare it without meat, which means diners derive their protein from a legume that's served alongside.

One day at my Italian restaurant, Trentina, I decided to whip up family meal for my staff before another busy evening. In the mad, crazed fit of preparing this salad, I happened to notice a chunk of bottarga, which are the salted and dried eggs of mullet or tuna, on a cutting board. Seeing that I loved bottarga and this salad, I figured why not add it to my final dish. The decision changed my life, and I haven't been able to envision this recipe without the addition of these luxurious fish eggs since then. You can source bottarga from any Italian market or reputable high-end grocery chain, like Whole Foods.

1 Rinse the lentils under cold running water. In a large bowl, combine the lentils and 1 quart water and let soak for a couple of minutes. Remove and discard anything that floats, and then drain.

2 In a medium stockpot over high heat, combine 2 cups water, the lentils, vinegar, red wine, and stock mirepoix and bring to a boil. Turn the heat to medium-low and simmer until the lentils are cooked through, about 30 minutes; their texture should be fork-tender.

3 Remove the pot from the heat and let cool for 30 minutes to 1 hour (no longer), then remove as much of the mirepoix as possible. Season aggressively with salt and

½ teaspoon pepper. Let sit for a couple minutes, then cover and transfer to the refrigerator for up to 4 days.

4 In a medium bowl, combine the lentils with the salad mirepoix, 1 tablespoon of the parsley, ¼ cup of the vinaigrette, and ½ teaspoon pepper; season with salt; and stir to mix. In another bowl, combine the frisée, bottarga, and 2 tablespoons vinaigrette and season with salt and pepper. Fold in the remaining 1 tablespoon parsley.

5 Divide the lentils among two plates and top each serving with the bread crumbs, a poached eggs or bacon, and the remaining vinaigrette as desired. Serve immediately.

SIMPLY DELICIOUS SALAD

Repeat after me: Salad can be both stupid-delicious and stupid-simple to make. Your lettuce and vinaigrette just need to meet some flavor and texture bombs in the forms of fruits, nuts, cheese, herbs, bread crumbs, and so on. Here are some simple combinations from around the world that are standard additions to a base of lettuce (any kind of lettuce is fine).

JAPANESE-AMERICAN	LEBANON	MIDDLE ITALY	SOUTHERN FRANCE	SPAIN
yuzu	mint	tomato	dried prune plum	apple
+	+	+	+	+
whipped tofu	tomato	provolone piccante	Époisses de Bourgogne cheese	Manchego
+	+	+	+	+
sesame	za'atar	pine nuts	black walnuts	Marcona almonds
+	+	+	+	+
shiso	toasted pita	bread crumbs	thyme	parsley
+	+		+	+
soy	labneh		rillettes	paprika

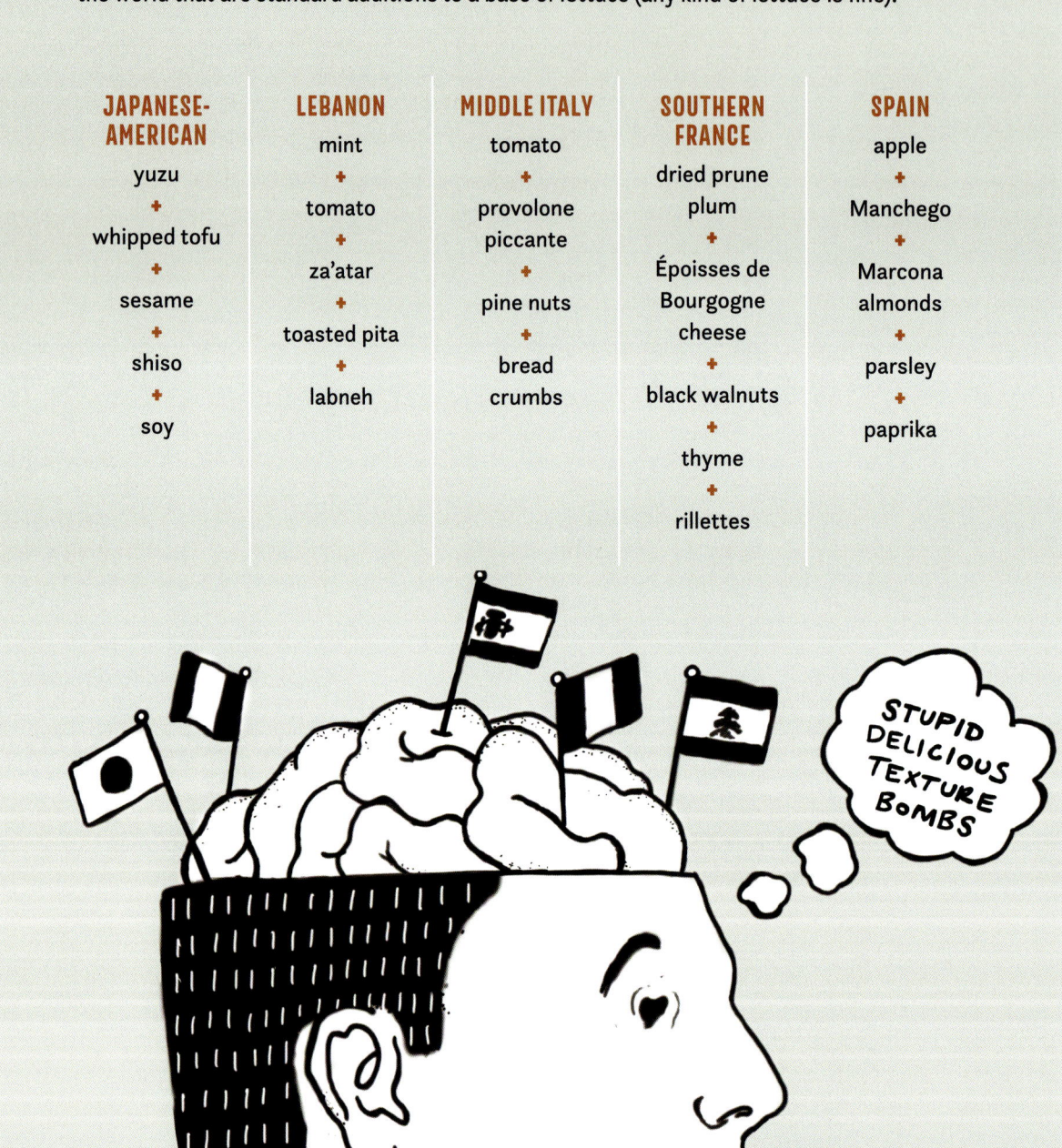

CLASSIC MAPLE VINAIGRETTE

Makes about 3 cups

2 cups blended oil (see page 22)

½ cup Apple Cider Vinegar (page 35)

¼ cup maple syrup

½ shallot, diced fine

1 teaspoon kosher salt

¼ teaspoon freshly ground pepper

Zest and juice of 2 lemons

Every chef-driven restaurant in America and Western Europe has a standard vinaigrette, and probably a stable of derivations based upon seasonal and local produce. Most chefs use a lemon vinaigrette, as I used to make with my buddy and fellow chef Michael Symon. However, many classically trained chefs prefer a sherry-shallot vinaigrette, and the Japanese love the *yuzu kosho* (a spicy citrus condiment that is a Japanese pantry necessity) or an old-school sushi restaurant classic that combines carrot, ginger, and miso. In any case, a vinaigrette recipe is a staple that's easy to whip up on a weekend and use all over the place. Once you master the basics, you can experiment and make it your own. Here's my go-to so that you have a head start on creating your own.

A word of caution: From my experience, the more aggressively you stir the vinaigrette—thereby raising its temperature—the more bitter it will become, especially if you're using appliances. However, if you're blending by hand, I've never found this to be an issue. To get a better sense about how to emulsify at home, consult the box on page 91.

In a medium bowl, combine the oil, vinegar, maple syrup, shallot, salt, pepper, lemon zest, and lemon juice and gently blend with a fork. Once finished, transfer in an airtight, nonreactive container. The vinaigrette will keep, in a cool, dark place, for up to 1 month.

VARIATION If you're feeling posh (or, as François Payard would say, "Make it nice or make it twice—make it *soigné*"), first cook the shallot in a pan over medium-low heat with some oil, salt, and pepper. Let cool, and then combine with the ingredients as directed.

 RETURN TO PAGE *95*

SQUASH SALAD

Serves 2 to 4

2 cups thinly sliced delicata squash

1 cup Classic Maple Vinaigrette (page 95)

1 teaspoon freshly ground pepper

Kosher salt

2 tablespoons salted cultured butter

1 bunch sage

1 tablespoon toasted, salted pumpkin seeds

2 apples (preferably late-ripening GoldRush apples)

1 lemon wedge

1 bunch watercress, leafy mustard greens, or arugula

¼ cup fresh, unflavored chèvre

1 teaspoon pumpkin-seed oil

Nutmeg for grating

Let's be clear: Fall and winter are fine times to have a salad. Even though not everyone has the pleasure of living year-round on the Amalfi Coast (a region on Italy's Sorrentine Peninsula that's known for its stunning seaside views and temperate weather), you can still grab grade-A seasonal vegetables, like squash, apples, beets, and celery root, to make a refreshing late-year salad. Although this recipe calls for delicata squash, any peeled tender, sweeter squash, like kabocha, acorn, or Blue Hubbard, will work, too. You just need to make sure that whatever squash you use is seeded and sliced paper-thin. If you're feeling ambitious, you can scoop out the squash seeds, toast them, and substitute them for the pumpkin seeds.

1   In a large ziplock bag, combine the squash, ¼ to ½ cup of the vinaigrette, and the pepper and season with salt. Let marinate for at least 1½ hours or up to 6 hours; this will tenderize and season the fall vegetable.

2   Preheat the oven to 350°F. Line a plate with a double thickness of paper towel.

3   In a small ovenproof sauté pan over low heat, melt 1 tablespoon of the butter. Add the sage, toss, and then season with salt. Place the pan in the oven and toast until the sage is crispy, 7 to 8 minutes. Carefully remove the sage and transfer to the prepared plate to drain. In the same pan, over low heat, melt the remaining 1 tablespoon butter. Add the pumpkin seeds and toss. Place the pan in

the oven and toast until crispy, 7 to 8 minutes. Transfer to pumpkin seeds to the plate with the sage, and let sit until both come to room temperature.

4   Meanwhile, core and cut the apples into paper-thin slices (about ⅛ inch), and rub them lightly with the lemon wedge to prevent oxidation. Set aside.

5   In a medium bowl, combine the remaining ¾ to ½ cup vinaigrette, the squash, and apples. Use your hands to toss the mixture, and then to fold in the watercress.

6   Smear individual plates with the chèvre, top each with the apple-squash salad, and garnish with the sage, pumpkin seeds, a drizzle of pumpkin-seed oil, and a grating of nutmeg. Serve immediately.

CHIMICHURRI

Makes about 1 quart

2 cups neutral oil (grapeseed, safflower, and canola all work)

2 cups chopped parsley, both leaves and stems

1 cup chopped cilantro, both leaves and stems

3 tablespoons rice vinegar (see variation, page 34)

2 teaspoons minced garlic

2 teaspoons diced red onion

1 small jalapeño chile, stemmed and seeded

Zest and juice of 1 lime

Kosher salt and freshly ground pepper

People know Argentina for its live-fire cooking, mountains, gauchos, wine, Lionel Messi, and general badassery, but this condiment is also synonymous with the country. You'll find it (and by *it*, I mean some local derivation of chimichurri) at every kitchen table, fire pit, fly-fishing lean-to, and restaurant in the country. We've consulted the recipes of Patagonian cooking legend Francis Mallmann and André Lima de Luca to adapt our own versions. These two Argentines are true modern-day renaissance men whose love of life, ingredient worship, and wood should inform your journeys with chimichurri. Enjoy the chimichurri with a pork chop (see page 104) or a nice strip steak.

In a food processor, combine the oil, parsley, cilantro, vinegar, garlic, onion, jalapeño, lemon zest, and lemon juice and then season with salt and pepper. Pulse until smooth, then transfer to an airtight container. The chimichurri will keep, refrigerated, for up to 2 weeks.

42ND & LE JEUNE MOJO SAUCE

Makes about 1 quart

2 sour oranges

½ red onion, thinly sliced

¼ cup chopped parsley, both leaves and stems

¼ cup chopped cilantro, both leaves and stems

¼ cup sliced mint leaves

2 teaspoons thinly sliced garlic

2 teaspoons ground cumin

Kosher salt and freshly ground pepper

2 cups neutral oil (grapeseed, safflower, and canola, all work)

2 tablespoons Apple Cider Vinegar (page 35)

When I was an intern at the Biltmore Hotel in Miami, I lived on Southwest 42nd Avenue (aka Le Jeune Road), just outside the vibrant streets of the Cuban neighborhood called Little Havana. Besides Cuban-style sandwiches and café con leche, pork with minty, tangy mojo sauce was one of my favorite food combinations in this historic enclave. You can also pair this sauce with plantain, yuca, or *ropa vieja* (a Cuban-style beef stew).

In order to keep the mint from oxidizing to black in mere moments, finely slice the same herb twice both lengthwise and widthwise. And the inclusion of "sour oranges" isn't a typo. You can find these delicious fruits at Spanish and Latin markets.

1 Zest the oranges and set it aside. Cut off both ends of each orange to expose the segments. Rest the citrus on a cutting board on one cut end and use a knife to remove, from top to bottom, the pith and any remaining peel. Hold the peeled citrus in your hand and carefully use the knife to separate the segments from the membrane surrounding them; set the segments aside. Finally, squeeze the pulp and membranes over a small bowl to extract any remaining juice. Discard the pulp and membranes.

2 In a food processor, combine the onion, parsley, cilantro, mint, garlic, and cumin and season with salt and pepper. Pulse several times to mix, then transfer to a medium bowl. (The mixture will start to darken within an hour.)

3 As close to serving time as possible, add the oil and vinegar to the bowl and stir to mix; the acidity in the liquid will oxidize the sauce—and you want to avoid that. Fold in all of the orange zest, segments, and juice. The mojo will keep, refrigerated, for up to 4 weeks, but will darken in color, losing its bright green hue.

ITALIAN SALSA VERDE

Makes about 1 pint

1½ cups chopped parsley, both leaves and stems

1 bunch oregano, leaves picked and chopped

2 sprigs thyme, leaves picked

⅔ cup "gold standard" olive oil (see page 23)

Kosher salt and freshly ground black pepper

¼ cup capers, chopped, with their brine

2 tablespoons white wine vinegar (see variation, page 34)

2 teaspoons minced garlic

2 teaspoons minced shallot

1 teaspoon red pepper flakes

Zest and juice of ½ lemon

Salsa verde, aka green sauce (and not to be confused former Cleveland Browns quarterback Vinny Testaverde), is a recipe that every modern chef should have memorized. It's multipurpose, and there's almost nothing where utilizing it doesn't make sense, whether you're making pork chops (see page 104) on a Monday night or braising beef ribs on a Sunday afternoon.

My personal come-to-Jesus moment with this salsa verde came when I was living in Rome with my uncle who works for the papacy. We were enjoying a simple grilled fish as a part of an extended outdoor Roman lunch when a chopped-up oily green thing appeared on the table. As I enjoyed my first bite of whole grilled fish and salsa verde, a taste memory of the herby accompaniment etched itself into my culinary mind. This Roman broken vinaigrette sauce is as versatile as they come.

In a food processor, combine the parsley, oregano, thyme, and olive oil and season with salt and black pepper. Pulse until it becomes a fine pesto-like paste. Add the capers and their brine, vinegar, garlic, shallot, red pepper flakes, lemon zest, and lemon juice and season with salt and pepper. Pulse several times until the mix looks homogenous and uniform, then transfer to an airtight container. The salsa verde will keep, refrigerated, for up to 2 weeks.

GRILLED SALSA VERDE

Makes about 2½ cups

⅔ cup "gold standard" olive oil (see page 23)

¼ cup capers, chopped, with their brine

2 tablespoons white wine vinegar (see variation, page 34)

2 teaspoons minced garlic

2 teaspoons minced shallot

2 sprigs thyme, leaves picked

1 teaspoon red pepper flakes

Zest and juice of ½ lemon

Kosher salt and freshly ground black pepper

1 bunch parsley

1 bunch oregano

Chef David Kocab, our former chef at Trentina in Cleveland, made this smoky version of salsa verde from the wood-fired hearths in our kitchen. It's amazing what just one additional simple step—grilling ingredients—can do to a sauce. Use this salsa liberally, especially when you don't want to head outside to put your dinner ingredients over a fire. It'll enhance any dish with a wood-roasted, rustic flavor.

1 Preheat the grill (or the broiler) to high.

2 In a medium bowl, combine the olive oil, capers and their brine, vinegar, garlic, shallot, thyme, red pepper flakes, lemon zest, and lemon juice and season with salt and black pepper.

3 Brush both bunches of parsley and oregano with the oil-caper mixture. Place the herbs in nice bundles (either tied or not) on the grill (or under the broiler) until charred, about 5 minutes. Be careful not to ignite the oil-caper mixture while charring the herbs.

4 Remove the herb bundles from the heat and chop them, including all the charred bits. Let cool and then combine with the remaining oil-caper mixture. The resulting sauce should be black in color.

5 Transfer to an airtight container. The salsa verde will keep, refrigerated, for up to 2 weeks.

BONE-MARROW SALSA VERDE

Makes about 3 cups

1½ cups chopped
parsley leaves
and stems

1 cup freshly grated
horseradish

⅔ cup beef bone marrow

¼ cup capers, chopped,
with their brine

2 tablespoons white
wine vinegar (see
variation, page 34)

2 teaspoons
minced garlic

1 teaspoon freshly
ground pepper

1 fresh white habanero
or ½ Scotch bonnet
chile, stemmed and
seeded

2 sprigs dill

Zest of 2 lemons

Kosher salt

I was trying to get an elegant, Italian-like caviar dish on the menu at Trentina when I first attempted this salsa. The combination of caviar and bone marrow just makes sense, and there's no better way to accent it than with a killer salsa verde that balances the opposing flavors of fatty, umami-rich beef bone marrow and tangy lemon-vinegar garlic. It's a raw sauce, however, so it needs to be cooked before serving. Crack some oysters or halve some fresh tomatoes, spoon this baller sauce on top, broil on high until the sauce is cooked through (about 3 minutes), then top with caviar. It's a winning meal.

In a food processor, combine the parsley, horseradish, bone marrow, capers and their brine, vinegar, garlic, pepper, chile, dill, and lemon zest and season with salt. Pulse until smooth, then transfer to an airtight container. The salsa verde will keep, refrigerated, for up to 3 days; or frozen for up to 6 months.

MONDAY-NIGHT PORK CHOPS WITH SALSA VERDE

Serves 2

2 boneless pork-loin chops, about 12 ounces total, with the fat cap on and minimum trimming

2 tablespoons kosher salt

1 tablespoon freshly ground black pepper

1 tablespoon freshly ground coriander

1 teaspoon red pepper flakes

1 teaspoon animal fat of your choice (such as beef, bacon, chicken, or duck)

Salsa verde of your choice (see pages 98 to 103) for serving

You can pair this pork chop with any of the five aforementioned green sauces, all of which have played special roles in my culinary career. If you want to match the seasonings on your pork to the seasoning of your sauce, think about the origin of the spices. So, in place of, or in addition to, the coriander in this version, use cumin for a Cuban pork chop with mojo (see page 99), or fennel for a pork chop with Italian Salsa Verde (page 100).

1   Using a knife, make shallow, ¼-inch-thick cuts in a diamond pattern on the fatty side of each loin chop.

2   Season the pork with the salt, black pepper, coriander, and red pepper flakes. Transfer to a glass baking dish or plate and let it rest at room temperature for 30 minutes.

3   Preheat the oven to 350°F.

4   Pat dry the flesh and fat on the chop, to ensure even cooking, leaving as much seasoning on the chop as possible.

5   Put the chops, fat-side down, in a cold 12-inch cast-iron skillet, place over medium heat, and sear the chops for 5 minutes. Then, crank the heat to high and cook until the fat side is rendered and a dark mahogany brown color, 3 to 5 minutes. Add the animal fat, flip the chops to the opposite flesh side, and immediately place the skillet into the oven until cooked through, 3 to 5 minutes more.

6   Remove the skillet from the oven and baste the chops with some of the fat that has accumulated in the pan. Transfer the chops to a plate, dress with salsa verde, and let them rest for up to 10 minutes. Slice the chops as desired and then dress again with more salsa verde. Serve immediately.

CHILE-PEACH WING SAUCE

Makes about 1 quart

4 very ripe peaches

6 fresh Fresno chiles, stemmed, seeded, and diced, or 1 cup sambal oelek

3 garlic cloves, smashed and peeled

2 tablespoons peeled and grated fresh ginger

Zest and juice of 4 limes

1 cup Tabasco sauce, plus more as needed

¼ cup soy sauce

¼ cup House Ketchup (page 78) or your favorite store-bought brand

¼ cup rice vinegar (see variation, page 34), plus more as needed

Kosher salt and freshly ground pepper

1 tablespoon wildflower honey (optional; use only if the peaches aren't ripe and/or sweet enough)

What makes this sauce so powerful is the base-ingredient combination of spicy chiles, sour lime and vinegar, and sweet tree-ripened fruit; we use very ripe, almost mushy peaches, but ripe pears, plums, and apples work equally well. (Add a splash of honey to the sauce to sweeten less-than-ripe fruit.) The sauce requires no cooking, and you can refrigerate it for months. We advocate making a large quantity so it can become your new go-to hot sauce on anything and everything (like ribs, burgers, eggs, and so on).

In a blender, combine the peaches, chiles, garlic, ginger, lime zest, lime juice, and Tabasco sauce. Puree until smooth and homogenous. Add the soy sauce, ketchup, and vinegar; season with salt and pepper; and puree to combine. Taste and adjust the seasoning with the honey and/ or vinegar, Tabasco, and salt until you have a sauce that's sweet, tangy, spicy, and salty. Transfer to an airtight container. The wing sauce will keep, refrigerated, for up to 4 months.

 RETURN TO PAGE *107*

SPICY PEACH CONFIT CHICKEN WINGS

Serves 4 or 5

½ cup kosher salt

¼ cup firmly packed natural brown sugar

2 teaspoons red pepper flakes

2 pounds all-natural, free-range chicken wings

1 gallon fry oil

2 cups Chile-Peach Wing Sauce (page 107)

To be honest, the Greenhouse Tavern's wings are the best chicken wings in America, and have been for years. When we opened the restaurant, we wanted to do duck confit, offering the classic French bistro dish (as well as others) through our American lens. The crispy confit chicken wing, done in the style of duck confit (duck legs cured and slowly cooked in their own fat), just made so much sense when we first tasted them. We knew they'd never leave the menu. These rich, sticky wings changed our perspective about what the venerable finger food could be.

Like all our deep-fried foods, we use rendered animal fat, preferably from cow, chicken, or duck. If you'd like to do the same, ask your butcher or grocer about buying some.

1 In a large bowl, combine the salt, brown sugar, and red pepper flakes; using your hands, thoroughly combine them.

2 Add the chicken wings to the bowl and thoroughly toss, again using your hands, to coat. Cover the bowl and refrigerate for 24 to 48 hours.

3 When ready to cook the wings, preheat the oven to 300°F, line a baking sheet with parchment paper, and line a plate with a double thickness of paper towel. Set aside.

4 Remove the chicken wings from the salt mixture, shaking off any excess. Place the wings in a deep roasting pan and pour in enough of the fry oil to completely cover them. Bake until the meat begins to separate from the bones, 2 to 3 hours. Using a slotted spoon, remove the wings from the oil, spread them on the prepared baking sheet, and let cool, 1 to 2 hours.

5 Carefully strain out and discard any solids from the used oil, then put the oil into a stockpot and set over medium heat until it reaches 400°F on a deep-fry thermometer.

6 Working in batches so as not to crowd the pot, cook the wings in the hot oil until golden and crispy, 4 to 5 minutes. Remove them with a slotted spoon and transfer to the prepared plate to drain.

7 In a large bowl, combine the wings with the wing sauce and toss to coat. Serve immediately.

RED WINE VINEGAR SOUBISE

Makes about 3 cups

4 large white onions, peeled and julienned

Kosher salt

1 pound unsalted butter

1½ teaspoons diced raw or roasted Fresno chile

¾ cup Old-School Red Wine Vinegar (page 34)

Soubise is a very traditional white sauce that is based on béchamel, one of the mother sauces that form the foundation of French cuisine. For us and our version, we wanted to pay homage to the traditional recipe as well as the new school. We figured we could use the tradition of super-slow-cooked onions with bracingly acidic vinegar to create a great onion sauce. But, unlike the traditional recipe, we didn't feel the need to stud the onion with cloves or base it on béchamel; all we care about is the onion itself. When whipped up, ours includes the perfect amount of onion, butter, and vinegar. What results (sometimes resembling mayo) can be used on anything at any temperature, whether it's slathered on a sandwich or placed next to a cut of fish.

1 In a large bowl, combine the onions and 3 teaspoons salt and toss to coat.

2 In a 4-quart Dutch oven or stockpot over medium heat, melt the butter. Add the onions and stir until they are evenly coated. Turn the heat as low as it can go, and cover the onions with the pot lid or a cartouche. Cook for 3 hours, removing the lid and stirring the onions occasionally. During this time, the onions must not receive any color or caramelize. Then, remove the onions from the heat and stir in the chile.

3 Transfer the contents of the pot to a blender and puree. With the motor running, stream the vinegar into the vortex created in the center of the mixture, then season with salt. Enjoy immediately or transfer to an airtight container. The soubise will keep, refrigerated, for up to 1 week. Serve cold or warm (reheat gently in a double boiler).

 RETURN TO PAGE _109_

CHOCOLATE DEVILS ON HORSEBACK

Makes 8 pieces

8 slices bacon

8 large dates, split open and pits removed

3 tablespoons chile paste

4 tablespoons coarsely chopped dark chocolate (70% cacao)

8 Marcona almonds

¼ cup Red Wine Vinegar Soubise (page 109)

Zest of 1 lemon

Red pepper flakes for garnish

Devils on Horseback is classic British fare that takes pitted dates and stuffs them with almonds and chiles and then wraps everything in bacon. The whole sticky, sweet, smoky, spicy mess is perfect for chasing down pints. In 2008, when I was still at Bar Cento, we partnered with the Cleveland Museum of Natural History to tackle the evolution of chocolate. I didn't want to do mole or anything obvious, so I tackled something that never had chocolate in it: Devils on Horseback. I knew the only other element needed to set it over the top was the addition of soubise, which would add a necessary acidic element to balance out the fatty recipe I'd concocted in my head.

It was a smashing success, and nothing many people had tasted before. After we first introduced it on the Greenhouse Tavern menu, we never looked back—we liked it that much. Each ingredient is there for a reason. Devils on Horseback, chocolate, and soubise complement one another perfectly.

1 Preheat the oven to 350°F. Line a baking sheet with parchment paper.

2 Lay the bacon on the prepared baking sheet and then bake until it's almost crispy yet still flexible, about 10 minutes. Transfer the bacon to another baking sheet and let cool to room temperature. Drain off the fat.

3 Increase the oven temperature to 400°F.

4 Place a split date on top of each slice of bacon with the split facing up. Stuff 1 teaspoon chile paste, one-eighth of the chocolate, and an almond in the center of each date.

Close each date over the filling and wrap tightly with the bacon slice. Skewer them with toothpicks to keep the bacon attached to the date and for easy eating later.

5 Bake the wrapped dates until the bacon is brown and crispy, about 5 minutes. Then, keeping the baking sheet in the oven, turn the broiler to high for 2 minutes to finish.

6 Meanwhile, in a small saucepan over low heat, warm the soubise.

7 Garnish each "devil" with about 1 tablespoon soubise, some lemon zest, and a pinch of red pepper flakes. Serve immediately.

XO À LA TRENTINA

Makes about 2 quarts

2 cups dried scallops

1 cup dried shrimp

¼ cup dried salted anchovies

1 cup dried white fungus

1 tablespoon Japanese seven spice (shichimi togarashi)

3 dried Thai bird chiles

1 piece whole mace

2 tablespoons coriander seeds

15 allspice berries

7 whole star anise

6 sheets nori

2 cups "silver standard" olive oil (see page 23)

1 cup diced country ham, Chinese ham, or prosciutto

½ cup diced Chinese dried sausage

½ cup diced beef jerky

½ cup diced bacon

1 cup peeled and diced fresh ginger

20 black garlic cloves or roasted garlic, peeled

1 large white onion, peeled and diced

3 cups tamari

2 cups Old-School Red Wine Vinegar (page 34)

10 fresh shiitake mushrooms, diced

2 cups fermented black beans

½ cup cooked black beans

Whether you realize it or not, food tastes better when there's umami in it. Umami, the fanciful and savory fifth taste, is commonly found in various forms throughout the world, such as fish sauce in Southeast Asia, garum in Roman cuisine, and XO sauce in China. In the case of XO sauce, specifically, the interplay of dried fish, mushrooms, cured meat, garlic, and other ingredients makes umami come alive. You'll find this sweet-and-sour condiment on noodles, fried rice, steamed buns, and steamed broccoli. At Trentina, we look at XO to help bolster the umami quotient in traditional Italian dishes like pasta, pizza, and salads.

Don't be intimidated by the lengthy ingredient list; you can find all of these things at a local Asian market. However, if you're not up for making this sauce, buy some prepared XO and skip ahead to the delicious bucatini recipe we've provided on page 115.

1 In a medium bowl, combine the scallops, shrimp, anchovies, and white fungus and add hot tap water to cover.

2 In a spice grinder or clean coffee grinder, and working in batches, coarsely grind the Japanese seven spice, chiles, mace, coriander seeds, allspice, star anise, and nori. Set aside.

3 In a slow cooker set to high, combine olive oil, ham, sausage, beef jerky, and bacon and render until the meat has turned golden brown, about 10 minutes. Be sure to stir occasionally to prevent burning. Add the ginger, garlic, and onion; cover; and cook until dark brown and completely broken down, about 1 hour. You'll need to stir occasionally to prevent burning.

4 Add the ground spices; seafood, fungus, and soaking liquid; tamari; vinegar; shiitakes; and both the fermented and cooked black beans to the slow cooker. Turn the heat to low, cover, and cook for a minimum of 2 hours or up to 10 hours; the sauce should look like a rustic, broken vinaigrette. Let cool, then transfer to an airtight container and put in the refrigerator to age for 3 days before using. The XO will keep, refrigerated, for up to 6 months.

 RETURN TO PAGE *112*

BUCATINI

Serves 2

BRODO

1 gallon water

2 cups stock mirepoix (see page 24) or mirepoix scraps

1 cup herb stems (any herbs you have, but I prefer parsley, thyme, and oregano for this)

5 fresh bay leaves

1 tablespoon white wine vinegar (see variation, page 34)

¼ cup mixed dried mushrooms

Freshly ground pepper

1 cup dry pasta (see Note)

½ cup chopped Parmesan or pecorino cheese rinds

1 pound bucatini pasta

1 tablespoon "gold standard" olive oil (see page 23)

1 garlic clove, sliced

2 tablespoons XO à la Trentina (page 112)

1 cup finely grated Parmesan cheese, plus more for serving

2 tablespoons unsalted butter

3 tablespoons bread crumbs (see page 27)

Freshly ground pepper

Sometimes you crave garlic-and-olive-oil pasta because *I'm super drunk and I need to eat something* or *I just woke up and I have only three things in my cupboard*. It's the ultimate lazy-man recipe, just like pasta *aglio e olio*, but with XO sauce, brodo, bucatini, and Parmesan in your pantry, this recipe is only minutes away.

1 To make the brodo: In a large stockpot, combine the water, mirepoix, herb stems, bay leaves, vinegar, and mushrooms and season with pepper. Top with the pasta and then the cheese rinds. (Because these two ingredients could stick and/or burn during the cooking process, put them on top and don't stir.) Set over high heat and bring to a boil, then turn the heat to medium-high and simmer for 2 hours. Remove from the heat and let cool to room temperature. Strain (discarding the solids) and reserve 1 cup of the brodo. Transfer the remaining brodo to an airtight container and store in the refrigerator for up to 1 week, or in the freezer for up to 2 months.

2 Bring a large pot of salted water to a boil. Add the pasta and cook until it is al dente, about 7 minutes (or until the manufacturer says it'll finish). When in doubt, take a bite of a noodle; it should be cooked but not toothy, not raw and not mush.

3 While the pasta is cooking, in a large sauté pan over medium-high heat, warm the olive oil. Add the garlic and sauté until it's cooked

through and golden in color, about 3 minutes. Add the XO sauce and cook for an additional minute. Add the reserved brodo, turn the heat to medium, and simmer for 1 to 2 minutes.

4 Once the pasta is cooked, drain the noodles—reserving ½ cup of the pasta water. Add the pasta and reserved pasta water to the sauce and cook for 1 to 2 minutes. Turn off the heat, move the pan to a cooler area (like an unused burner), and fold in the Parmesan and butter until they're well combined. Be aware that if the sauce encounters too much heat during this step, it will break (i.e., it won't emulsify).

5 Divide the pasta among two bowls and garnish with the bread crumbs and additional Parmesan, and season with pepper. Serve immediately.

NOTE Any pasta will do here, as you're not going to eat the actual pasta; the inclusion of the pasta just provides body to the broth.

4

BRINING, MARINATING & BRAISING

When you brine, marinate, or braise something, it's not yet perfect. When you're talking about these techniques, you're taking ugly veggies and unsexy cuts of meat—the *cucina povera*, as the Italians would call it, aka peasant food—and transforming them into world-class dishes in their own right. In culinary school, way before I owned restaurants and had a family, I'd make sausage or corned beef from these less-desirable foods. It's an insanely simple way to turn the mundane into a celebration that everyone can rally around. Within this chapter, I'm going to hand you the keys to unlocking the hidden potential within underappreciated meat cuts and vegetables.

Before we dive in, let's answer this question (because it's obviously central to this entire book): Why is vinegar important to brining, marinating, and braising? Simple. Vinegar is what tenderizes and flavors. It's the catalyst to breaking down these tough throwaway pieces.

When we brine, we utilize a basic ratio (with some slight fluctuations) of 1 gallon of water, ½ cup of sugar, ½ cup of salt, and a mix of herbs and spices to allow water and flavor to flow back and forth between a piece of meat and its brine. What sets brining apart from pickling (another vinegar-based technique that we explore starting on page 47), is brining typically extends the shelf life of meat, whereas pickling concerns preserving damn-near everything else. Be aware that many brining recipes need to be started 24 to 48 hours in advance for curing, so preplanning is necessary.

When we marinate and braise, we use a bunch of flavorful stuff to break down the collagen, tough muscles, and insoluble fats within meat, or to tenderize the fibers within carrots and other vegetables. When it comes to selecting the proper meat cuts to marinate and braise, remember this: You want to select a piece of the animal from close to the ground, as it'll be more flavorful but not as tender; for example, you wouldn't just grill a shank because it'd be impossibly tough to eat. That's why they're called the butcher's cuts of meat. It's also why Sunday Gravy over Cavatelli (page 135) is so delicious, and you love the beef short rib so much; you're taking a fully flavored cut and making it edible.

These recipes will teach you how to balance the flavors of rich brines, marinades, and braises while using vinegar. Let's get into it.

BRINED BEER-CAN CHICKEN
(AKA BEER-BUTT CHICKEN)

Serves 4

BEER-CAN CHICKEN BRINE

½ gallon warm water

1 cup diced salad mirepoix (see page 24)

⅔ cup kosher salt

½ cup firmly packed natural brown sugar

½ cup beer

½ cup Greenhouse Tavern–Style Craft-Beer Vinegar (page 32)

1 garlic head, smashed

4 fresh or dried bay leaves

½ gallon ice cubes

One 5-pound organic, pasture-raised chicken

6 tablespoons coarsely ground coriander seeds

4 tablespoons coarsely ground black peppercorns

2 tablespoons smoked paprika

2 tablespoons chili powder

1 tablespoon natural brown sugar

1 tablespoon kosher salt

1 teaspoon dried thyme

Three 12-ounce cans of beer (1 beer is for the chicken, the other 2 are for you to drink while cooking)

Zest and juice of 1 lemon

Because beer-can cooking has been stereotyped as something that Red America passionately champions, it's typically looked down upon; however, it's really just a great recipe for chicken that uses an ingredient that's more American than wine. Think of beer-can chicken as the American equivalent of French coq au vin.

The hook about this dish is that most recipes call for a quick marinade of salt, pepper, sugar, and maybe seasonings. These iterations essentially create a magic BBQ powder. Our recipe takes beer-can chicken to the next level, as we inject beer and beer vinegar into the brine. A pilsner, lager, or wheat beer with very little hops will do here; don't use an IPA or other hoppy beer. Your chicken brines and braises in your brew of choice, delivering not a beer-tasting concoction but a tender, moist, and roasted piece of poultry. I know it's super-easy to buy an already-roasted chicken at the grocery store (nothing wrong with that!), but beer-can chicken will cost you one-fifth of the roasted chicken, and you can make your own stock afterward. Plus, you'll have the added benefit of saying you actually cooked it. And remember the mantra: Don't just drink beer; cook with it.

1 To make the brine: In a large stainless-steel stockpot over high heat, combine the water, mirepoix, salt, brown sugar, beer, vinegar, garlic, and bay leaves. Bring to a boil and stir to dissolve the salt and sugar, about 5 minutes. Remove the brine from the heat and let cool to room temperature.

2 Transfer the brine to a nonreactive bowl or large heavy-duty ziplock bag and add the ice to cool the temperature to below 40°F (approximate refrigerator temperature). Add the chicken to the brine, making sure it is completely submerged. Transfer the chicken and brine to the refrigerator and let it sit for at least 12 or up to 24 hours.

3 Preheat the grill to medium-high or a smoker or oven to 350°F.

4 Remove the chicken from the brine and pat it dry with paper towels. Discard the brine.

CONTINUED

5 In a bowl, combine the coriander seeds, peppercorns, paprika, chili powder, brown sugar, salt, and thyme. Dust the entire bird inside and out with the mixture.

6 Open all three beers, chug two (this is essential), and reserve one for the chicken.

7 Stand the remaining full beer can straight up in a metal pie tin, place the chicken's butt on top of the can (I hate to be crass, but that's essentially what the cavity is), and push the chicken down to fully insert the can. In theory, this will stabilize the chicken to "stand" upright on its legs and thighs. (You can buy great pans and trays to hold your chicken in place of the can, or you can simply use foil; however, we suggest using a can for its kitschy aspect.)

8 Place the pie tin on the grill and cook the chicken to an internal temperature of 165°F, about 1½ hours. The goal in letting the chicken cook longer than usual is that the outside pieces of the chicken receive the most direct heat, while the more-tender and leaner breast gets little direct heat.

9 Allow the bird to rest in the pan on the beer can for 10 minutes before carving.

10 Dress the chicken with 2 teaspoons of the beer and pan drippings, the lemon zest, and lemon juice. Serve immediately.

BRINED & BOILED CORNED LAMB & CABBAGE
(AKA POTÉE OR POT-AU-FEU)

Serves 8

CORNED LAMB BRINE

½ gallon warm water

1 cup diced stock mirepoix (see page 24)

⅔ cup kosher salt

½ cup firmly packed natural brown sugar

½ cup white wine vinegar (see variation, page 34)

1 tablespoon black peppercorns

1 tablespoon whole cloves

1 teaspoon curing salt #1 (see Note)

1 garlic head, smashed

1 bunch sage

1 bunch rosemary

4 fresh or dried bay leaves

½ gallon ice cubes

1 leg of lamb, about 5 pounds, boned and tied

2 quarts water

¼ cup white wine vinegar (see variation, page 34)

We love corning lamb because we have an abundance of the animal in Ohio, and it's also more flavorful and interesting than beef (the truth hurts, beef fans). To get technical for a second, let me explain what *corning* is. It's a technique that places either beef or lamb into a specifically seasoned brine, leaving it there long enough to cure all the way through and producing a piece of meat that looks like a fresh ham, pink and salty. This curing process ensures an evenly seasoned and tender cut because a salty osmosis, which occurs when the lamb is in the brine, changes the meat's cellular composition, drawing out its moisture.

This recipe requires at least seven days of corning and might require up to twenty-one days, depending on the size of your cut of meat (corning's a time-consuming technique, man). But once completed, it's good to hang out in the fridge for a while. Granted, it's not good forever, but if you cut it into pieces, it could last up to a month—or you can keep it in the freezer indefinitely. Employ for sandwiches or hash, or just eat the whole leg by yourself.

1   To make the brine: In a large stainless-steel pot over high heat, combine the water, mirepoix, kosher salt, brown sugar, vinegar, peppercorns, cloves, curing salt, garlic, sage, rosemary, and bay leaves. Bring to a boil and stir to dissolve the salt and sugar, about 5 minutes. Remove the brine from the heat and allow to cool to room temperature.

2   Transfer the brine to a nonreactive pot or large heavy-duty ziplock bag and add the ice to cool the temperature below 40°F (approximate refrigerator temperature). Add the lamb to the brine, making sure it is completely submerged, cover, and refrigerate for at least 7 days and up to 21 days; the longer the leg brines, the more tender and flavorful it'll be.

10 garlic cloves, peeled

1 tablespoon torn
fresh sage leaves

1 tablespoon chopped
fresh rosemary leaves

4 fresh bay leaves

1 teaspoon whole cloves

1 quart small potatoes
(preferably German
Butterball), left whole

1 cup baby carrots

1 cup whole pearl
onions, peeled

1 head napa cabbage,
cut into 1-inch-thick
wedges

Kosher salt

Zest of 1 lemon

3 Remove the lamb from the brine
and pat it dry with paper towels.
Discard the brine.

4 In a Dutch oven over low heat,
combine the lamb, water, vinegar,
garlic, half of the sage, half of
the rosemary, and the bay leaves.
Simmer, covered, until meat is
almost tender, about 2 hours. Add
the potatoes, carrots, and onions
and simmer until the carrots and
potatoes are fork-tender, 20 to
30 minutes. Add the cabbage and
simmer for 15 minutes more.

5 Remove the lamb from the stew
and place it on a cutting board; let
cool to room temperature. Then,
thinly slice the lamb crosswise, put
onto a serving platter, and dress
with about ½ cup of the braising
liquid. On a second serving platter,
place the cabbage, carrots, onions,
potatoes, and remaining sage and
rosemary and garnish with some
kosher salt and lemon zest. Serve
immediately.

NOTE Curing salt #1 is a salt that is
high in nitrites to ensure safety during
a long cure in brine; you can find it at
Amazon or any spice merchant.

BBQ PIG'S HEAD
(BRINED, BRAISED & ROASTED PIG WITH BBQ SAUCE)

Serves 4 to 6

BBQ PIG'S HEAD BRINE

½ gallon warm water

1 cup kosher salt

1 cup firmly packed natural brown sugar

1 cup Old-School Red Wine Vinegar (page 34)

½ cup soy sauce

½ cup red pepper flakes

¼ cup honey

One 12-ounce can cola

2 tablespoons ground coriander seeds

1 tablespoon dried thyme

1 tablespoon freshly ground black pepper

1 tablespoon Szechuan peppercorns

1 tablespoon sweet paprika

1 tablespoon chili powder

1 teaspoon cayenne pepper

½ gallon ice cubes

One 8- to 12-pound pig's head, split, with eyes, tongue, brains, and ears removed by your butcher and reserved

4 to 6 quarts water, depending on size of braising vessel

When we opened Greenhouse Tavern, the farmers we worked with weren't nearly as big as they are today. At the time, our butcher didn't even have a Cryovac machine, so we'd receive quarter or whole pieces of animal that we had to cook immediately, even if they weren't useful cuts. For comparison's sake, think about going to the farmers' market late and your butcher's out of all the prized stuff: loins, tenderloins, strips, and skirts. You look down and glimpse nothing but scraps. But at Greenhouse Tavern, we learned to embrace this exact SOL situation, as what's left behind typically begets a treasure trove. Actually, it's how we figured out our beloved BBQ pig's head recipe; it made us conceptualize an exceptional dish by utilizing nothing but the underloved cuts of pork. This ingenious creation helped revolutionize the way Americans eat pig. How sure I am of this claim? The price of head skyrocketed by 40 percent since we put it on the menu.

To be more specific, here's the anecdote behind how this recipe became a menu staple. After butchery, we were consistently left with pigs' heads and pigs' shanks, neither of which we could work into an entrée or sausage. But we wanted to find a use for them to tap into their fatty, delicious stature. So one weekend we challenged our patrons to a contest that would decide the cut of meat we'd focus on. We pitted a stuffed pig trotter (called a zampone) against a brined-and-braised barbecued pig's head. Within the first dinner service, we were out of pigs' heads. Ever since then, it's been a feature on the menu and an item that we sell out—so much so that we now buy the pigs' heads as a cut of meat.

1 To make the brine: In a large stainless-steel pot over high heat, combine the water, salt, brown sugar, vinegar, soy sauce, red pepper flakes, honey, cola, coriander, thyme, black pepper, peppercorns, paprika, chili powder, and cayenne. Bring to a boil and stir to dissolve the salt and sugar, about 5 minutes. Remove the brine from the heat and let cool to room temperature.

2 Transfer the brine to a nonreactive bowl or large heavy-duty ziplock bag and add the ice to cool the temperature below 40°F (approximate refrigerator

CONTINUED

One 750-ml bottle red wine

One to three 12-ounce cans cola, depending on size of braising vessel

1 cup honey

½ cup kosher salt

½ cup Old-School Red Wine Vinegar (page 34)

10 whole dried chiles

2 tablespoons black peppercorns

FACE BBQ SAUCE

3 tablespoons grapeseed oil

3 tablespoons sesame oil

1 tablespoon sesame seeds

2 teaspoons mustard powder

1 teaspoon peeled and grated fresh ginger

1 teaspoon minced garlic

1 cup soy sauce

1 cup honey

¼ cup sambal oelek

¼ cup House Ketchup (page 78)

¼ cup Apple Cider Vinegar (page 35)

4 brioche burger buns

1 head butter lettuce

2 cups thinly sliced raw vegetables, such as radish, carrot, bell pepper, and fennel

1 lime, cut into wedges

temperature). Place the pig's head into the brine, making sure it's fully submerged, and refrigerate, covered, for 48 hours.

3   Preheat the oven to 250°F.

4   After 48 hours, in a large saucepan over medium-high heat, combine the water, wine, cola, honey, salt, vinegar, chiles, and peppercorns. Bring the braising liquid to a boil, stirring occasionally until the honey is dissolved.

5   Remove the head from the brine and pat it dry with paper towels. Discard the brine. Place the head in a deep roasting pan, pour in the braising liquid until the head is partially covered, and cover the pan tightly with aluminum foil. Place the pig's head in the oven and cook for a minimum of 8 hours or up to overnight. When the head is tender to the touch, to the point where you could pull it apart, remove it from the oven and allow to cool in the braising liquid. Once the head and liquid have cooled to approximately 70°F (you should notice the rendered fat starting to solidify), place the whole roasting pan in the refrigerator to cool completely.

6   To make the BBQ sauce: In a sauté pan over medium heat, combine the grapeseed oil, sesame oil, sesame seeds, mustard powder, ginger, and garlic. Toast, stirring constantly, until the garlic is almost blackened, about 5 minutes. Remove the pan from the heat, put the mixture in

a blender, and set it aside until it's cool enough to touch. Then, thoroughly puree until smooth. Add the soy sauce, honey, sambal oelek, ketchup, and vinegar to the blender and blend until smooth. Measure out 1 cup for the recipe; transfer the remaining 2 cups to an airtight container and store in the refrigerator for up to 6 months.

7   Preheat the oven to 350°F.

8   Remove the pig's head from the braising liquid. Score the head in a grid pattern (cross-hatching) by cutting diagonal, diamond-shaped, 1-inch slits in it; this prevents the skin from puffing up while cooking and allows the fat to render and the skin to crisp.

9   Place 1 cup of the braising liquid in a large roasting pan, add the pig's head skin-side up, and cook in the oven for 30 minutes. Then, brush the head with BBQ sauce and return it to the oven for another 15 minutes. Repeat, brushing the pig's head with more BBQ sauce and returning to the oven for another 10 minutes to ensure it becomes super–dark brown and caramelized. Remove from the oven and let rest for 10 minutes.

10 Using a steak knife and tongs, pull off sticky, delicious pieces of pork and place it on buns topped with lettuce, sliced raw vegetables, and more BBQ sauce. Serve immediately with the lime wedges.

BONE-IN BEEF POT ROAST

Serves 4

POT ROAST BRINE

1 gallon warm water

1 cup diced salad mirepoix (see page 24)

⅔ cup kosher salt

½ cup firmly packed natural brown sugar

½ cup red wine

2 tablespoons Old-School Red Wine Vinegar (page 34)

1 garlic head, smashed

4 fresh or dried bay leaves

4 pounds beef shin, split

½ cup neutral oil

1 carrot, cut into 1-inch dice

1 large onion, cut into 1-inch dice

1 celery stalk cut into 1-inch dice

1 cup red wine

¼ cup Old-School Red Wine Vinegar (page 34)

4 fresh or dried bay leaves

4 sprigs thyme

2 sprigs rosemary

2 tablespoons black peppercorns

1 teaspoon allspice berries

1 to 4 quarts beef stock, depending on the size of your braising vessel

Some of my favorite childhood sandwiches involved meat left over from the previous day assembled atop that day's bread. These half-baked concoctions included everything from beef pot roast with all the fixin's to cold fried chicken to meat loaf to sauerbraten piled on the delicious pieces of sliced bread my parents always kept in the pantry. All I had to do was add some mayonnaise and—voilà!—I was done.

When I think of these dishes from yesteryear, the Greenhouse Tavern bone-in beef pot roast immediately comes to mind. It's been on the restaurant's menu since Day One. For many, the concept of subpar home-cooked pot roast stems from the fact that most people use the cheapest possible cut of meat. No joke, the grocery store wants you to select that lackluster eye of round or London broil for your pot roast. Personally, I don't have anything against these cuts—I would typically use them for a super-lean steak sandwich or my burger meat—but they're being used for the wrong purpose. For our recipe, the one that'll have you hearing angels blasting on trumpets each time the term *pot roast* is uttered, we recommend using a cut that will yield more fat, flavor, and texture, like shin, but short rib shank, cheek, shoulder, belly, or chuck roll can be substituted. One taste of pot roast from these flavorful treasures of the beast will make you forget the dry iteration that America has, unfortunately, grown used to.

Although this recipe uses a traditional brine, you can always substitute ½ gallon of warm water and ¾ gallon of ice for the gallon of warm water. It's quicker to dissolve the seasonings in a hot liquid, and adding ice chills the brine quicker. See Brined Beer-Can Chicken, page 121, for this technique.

1 To make the brine: In a large stainless-steel pot over high heat, combine the water, mirepoix, salt, brown sugar, wine, vinegar, garlic, and bay leaves. Bring to a boil and stir to dissolve the salt and sugar, about 5 minutes. Remove the brine from the heat.

2 Transfer the brine to a nonreactive bowl or large heavy-duty ziplock bag and refrigerate until its temperature is below 40°F (approximate refrigerator temperature). Add the beef shin, making sure it is completely submerged, cover, return to the refrigerator, and allow to brine for 24 to 48 hours.

POMMES PUREE

2 large Idaho potatoes, washed, skin on (the older and bigger, the better)

¼ cup cold unsalted butter, cubed

1 cup buttermilk

Kosher salt

Green sauce of your choice (see pages 98 to 103) for serving

3   Preheat the oven to 300°F for a 6-hour braise, or 250°F for an overnight braise.

4   Remove the shin from the brine and pat it dry with paper towels. Discard the brine.

5   In a large roasting pan or Dutch oven over medium-high heat, warm the oil. Add the beef and sear the shin on all sides in order to get a rich mahogany color. Remember, a darker color yields deeper flavor.

6   Once the shin has been fully seared, remove it and reserve for later. Turn the heat to medium; add the carrot, onion, and celery to the pan; and cook, stirring occasionally, until the vegetables have softened and taken on some color, 10 to 15 minutes. Add the wine and vinegar, turn the heat to high, and deglaze the pan, stirring to scrape up any browned bits with a wooden spoon.

7   Tie the bay leaves, thyme, rosemary, peppercorns, and allspice in a piece of cheesecloth to make a sachet; set aside.

8   When the liquid has almost completely reduced, return the beef shin to the pan, cover completely with the beef stock, and add the sachet. Bring to a simmer, cover first with parchment paper and then with aluminum foil or a lid. Transfer to the oven and braise at 300°F for 6 hours, or 250°F for 8 to 10 hours. Check to make

sure the shin is done—you should see the meat falling off the bone—before removing it from the oven. If necessary, continue to cook, checking periodically.

9   Strain three-fourths of the braising liquid into a separate container. Reserve the beef, veggies, and remaining liquid until you are ready to serve. (You can let the roast cool, uncovered, in the refrigerator, and then cover and keep refrigerated for up to 4 days. Reheat, uncovered, in a 350°F oven for 20 minutes.)

10   To make the pommes puree: In a large pot of salted water over high heat, bring the potatoes to a boil. Turn the heat to a simmer and then cook the potatoes until they are soft enough to easily pierce with a knife (but not mushy), about 45 minutes. (Do not use any potatoes that broke in the cooking process; they will be waterlogged and taste like it. Unfortunately, you'll need to start over.) Drain the potatoes and then peel them while they're still warm; if you let them cool, your pommes puree will be gummy. Discard the skins.

11   Put the peeled potatoes through a ricer or a food mill and then place them in a pot over very low heat to keep them hot. Mix in half of the butter and buttermilk until incorporated; then continue adding the remaining butter and

CONTINUED

buttermilk. Think of the puree as an emulsified vinaigrette: you need to stir the mixture each time as you incorporate more butter and buttermilk. Season with salt. Hold the puree in a low-temperature oven, covered, until you are ready to serve.

12   Pour the reserved braising liquid into a saucepan over medium-high heat. Reduce the liquid by more than half to make a sticky, rich sauce.

13   Slice the pot roast, transfer to individual plates along with the pommes puree, and then top with the reduced sauce and green sauce. Serve immediately.

NOTE   You can use a slow cooker for the pot roast. Following the method through deglazing the beef shin pan, then transfer everything to your slow cooker and cook on high for 6 hours, or on low for 8 to 10 hours.

SUNDAY GRAVY OVER CAVATELLI
(AKA A BIG OL' BOILING BATCH OF RED SAUCE)

Serves 6

1 pound pork spare ribs

1 pound beef neck bones, brisket, or shank

1 pound veal shank, sliced crosswise 1 inch thick (osso buco–style)

Kosher salt and freshly ground pepper

1 cup "silver standard" olive oil (see page 23)

2 cups small-diced stock mirepoix (see page 24)

¼ cup tomato paste

1 cup red wine

½ cup Old-School Red Wine Vinegar (page 34)

½ gallon tomato passato (see Note, page 162)

1 pound spicy Italian sausage

1 pound fresh ricotta cavatelli, prepared according to package instructions

½ cup grated Parmesan cheese

½ cup bread crumbs (see page 27)

1 bunch basil, leaves torn

Sunday gravy, red gravy, marinara, the sauce—whatever you call it, a huge, boiling pot of red sauce is awesome. Not only does it taste out-of-this-world fantastic—the sweet, tangy tomato sauce explodes with flavor when poured on everything from pasta to short ribs—but the tradition of making it is a total labor of love. Some nonnas I know start the sauce on Thursday for Sunday supper, allowing several different meats to slowly braise in the acidic stew. Other nonnas employ different tactics and superstitions, like only stirring clockwise or with a wooden spoon. But no matter how it's made, anyone attempting it needs to remember to stir regularly to prevent burning (however, starting four days ahead of time isn't really necessary).

Just remember, the only way to eat this wonder is with pasta, meats, bread, and salad on the side—oh, and don't let Uncle Paulie from *Goodfellas* catch you sneaking too many onions into the sauce.

1 Season the pork ribs, beef neck bones, and veal shank with salt and pepper, cover, and refrigerate for as little as 5 minutes or up to a full day, to ensure maximum tenderness once they're done cooking.

2 Preheat the oven to 300°F.

3 In a large ovenproof stainless-steel stockpot or Dutch oven over medium-high heat, warm ¾ cup of the olive oil. Add the meat in batches—pork ribs, neck bones, and then veal—and sear each batch until super–dark brown, about 7 minutes per side. After each meat is browned, remove it from the pot and reserve. Discard the cooking oil.

4 Add the remaining ¼ cup olive oil, the mirepoix, and tomato paste to the pot and season with salt and pepper. Cook over medium-high heat, covered, for 10 minutes, stirring often. Add the wine and vinegar, turn the heat to medium, and deglaze the pot, scraping up any browned bits with a wooden spoon. Then, add the tomato passato and bring to a simmer. Add the seared pork ribs, beef neck bones, and veal shank and place in the oven, uncovered, for 4 hours, stirring gently and scraping the sides and bottom of the pot every hour to prevent any burning.

CONTINUED

5 After 4 hours, remove the pot from the oven, add the sausage, and set over low heat on the stove top; simmer until you're ready to serve. Then, shut off the heat and allow everything to slowly cool to room temperature.

6 If your entire dinner party is present and hungry, simply transfer the meats and a little sauce to a platter for all to enjoy family-style. Toss the cavatelli with the remaining sauce, garnish with the Parmesan, bread crumbs, and basil; and serve. If your guests are joining you throughout the day, follow these steps to ensure the food and presentation remain as elegant and tasty as if your meal were fresh off the stove.

- Preheat the oven to 200°F.

- Transfer the pork ribs to a shallow 9 by 13-inch baking pan. Ladle some sauce on top, then cover with a lid or aluminum foil and hold it in the oven. Transfer the beef neck bones to another 9 by 13-inch baking pan, flake off the meat, discard the bones, ladle some sauce over, cover with a lid or foil, and hold in the oven. Transfer the veal shank to another 9 by 13-inch baking pan, flake off the meat, discard the bone, ladle some sauce over, cover with a lid or foil, and hold in the oven. Pull the sausage from the sauce and cut each link in half crosswise. Transfer the sausage to yet another 9 by 13-inch baking pan, cover with a lid or foil, and hold in the oven.

ETIQUETTE NOTES FROM A BRUTE WHO LOVES TRADITION

Eat your salad *after* your meal. Never use a side plate for scarpetta, aka the Italian bread you'll use for wiping your plate clean of the Sunday gravy. And do not put the meat into the pasta—place it on the side, which is how I was taught it's been done (right or wrong) for generations. Also, swill your red wine from a juice glass.

THE BEST ROOT-VEGETABLE ROAST OF YOUR LIFE

Serves 2

1 cup peeled and quartered baby yellow beets, tops trimmed to 1 inch

¼ cup grapeseed oil

Kosher salt and freshly ground pepper

1 cup ½-inch half-moon-sliced carrots

1 head fennel, cut into quarters

1 cup large-diced celery root

1 cup quartered small turnips

1 cup radishes

¼ cup brodo (see page 115), plus 1 tablespoon

2 tablespoons miso

1 tablespoon Apple Cider Vinegar (page 35)

1 tablespoon unsalted butter

Zest of 1 orange

2 tablespoons bread crumbs (see page 27)

Marinating shouldn't be used just for meats. It's also a great technique to season and tenderize veggies. This simple recipe allows you to throw vegetables into your brining and braising fun, too. Follow these steps to turn your idea of what vegetables can be on its head. Also, unlike the other recipes you've read so far in this chapter, we will roast, marinate, and then braise or roast the veggies again (essentially, we won't start with the braise). Prepare to have your mind blown. I prefer using beets that aren't red for this recipe, as red ones will stain the other ingredients. And if there are any leftovers, serve with lettuce and top with a hard-cooked egg, almonds, a vinaigrette, and some grated Parmesan for lunch the next day.

1 Preheat the oven to 350°F. Line a baking sheet with parchment paper.

2 In a medium bowl, toss the beets with one-third of the grapeseed oil to coat and season with salt and pepper. Spread the beets in an even layer on the prepared baking sheet and then roast for 10 minutes.

3 In the same bowl, toss the carrots with another one-third of the oil to coat and season with salt and pepper. Add to the beets and roast for 15 minutes more.

4 In the same bowl, toss the fennel, celery root, turnips, and radishes with the remaining oil to coat and season with salt and pepper. Add to the beets and carrots and roast for 20 minutes longer. When the vegetables are essentially al dente and still have a firm texture in the center, remove them from the oven. You want to undercook them now because they will finish cooking later.

5 Meanwhile, in a large bowl, combine the ¼ cup brodo, miso, and vinegar and whisk until homogeneous. Add all the hot al dente vegetables, making sure they are submerged, and let soak at room temperature for at least 30 minutes or up to 3 hours.

6 Preheat the oven to 350°F. Line a baking sheet with parchment paper.

7 Remove the vegetables from the marinade, discarding the marinade, and place on the prepared baking sheet. Roast for 10 minutes; the vegetables should now be fork-tender.

8 While the vegetables are still hot, place them in a large bowl and add the remaining 1 tablespoon brodo and the butter. Using tongs, toss the vegetables to melt and emulsify the butter. Transfer to a large serving platter and garnish with orange zest and bread crumbs. Serve immediately.

SCALLOP CRUDO

Serves 2

3 whole live U10
scallops

Zest and juice of
½ orange

Pinch of kosher salt

2 tablespoons
champagne vinegar or
white wine vinegar (see
variation, page 34)

1 tablespoon "gold
standard" olive oil
(see page 23)

¼ cup thinly sliced
fennel bulb, plus
1 tablespoon torn
fennel fronds

10 pink peppercorns,
crushed

1 tablespoon very finely
chopped pistachios

Zest of 1 lemon

Bottom line, you'll complete no recipe in this chapter quicker than this one because it's crudo, which is simply raw fish. Why is raw fish so easy to prepare? Fish take on marinades more quickly than meats or vegetables, so your prep time is less than if you were dealing with other proteins. This base recipe is intended for scallops, but it also works for clams, snapper, or any treasure of the ocean that you want to slurp down raw-ish. We, of course, always clean and butcher scallops ourselves because we use every bit of the shellfish. We love curing the roe sack for grating on pastas and preserving the foot to use in a raw mousseline. We also save the stomach and bile-producing digestive gland to make funk ferments like fish sauce or XO. Keep the rest of the parts to utilize in an XO sauce (see page 112) or to dry for stock. We clean the shells well and reserve them in the refrigerator for plating the crudo. If you're not confident in your cleaning and prep skills, have your fishmonger shuck and clean the scallops (but definitely take the roe sack home with you) or buy dry-packed, already-butchered scallops. In this case, we use size U10 (U meaning under, or fewer than, 10 scallops per 1 pound), but smaller bay scallops up to size U20 will work, too.

1 Discard each scallop's main muscle, called the adductor; it's a white hockey-puck-looking thing. Using a fillet knife, slice the scallops ¼ inch thick and place them in a bowl. Season with the orange zest, salt, vinegar, and olive oil, then allow them to marinate for 5 to 15 minutes on ice or in the refrigerator; any longer than that will fully cure the scallop, changing its flavor and texture.

2 Once marinated, gently toss the scallops with the sliced fennel and orange juice.

3 Evenly divide the sliced scallops and fennel among two chilled, cleaned reserved shells or serving plates, shingling (overlapping) them in a single layer. Garnish with the fennel fronds, top with a couple pinches of pink peppercorns, a sprinkle of pistachios, and the lemon zest. Serve immediately.

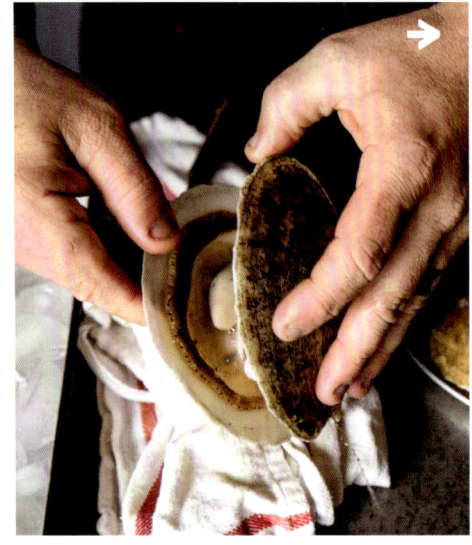
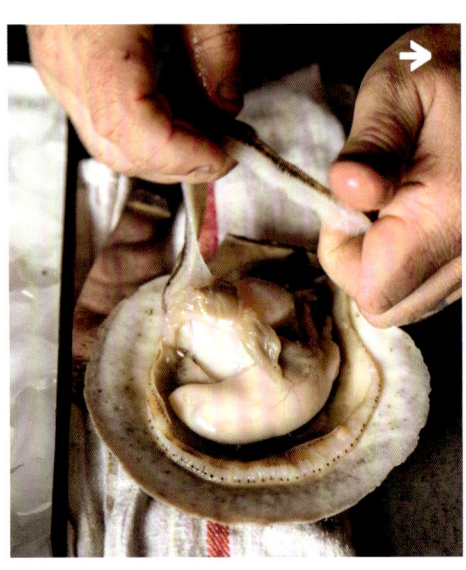

FRIED & MARINATED LAKE FISH IN SAOR

Serves 2

½ cup grapeseed oil, plus 1 tablespoon

¼ cup all-purpose flour

1 pound lake fish, preferably yellow perch, walleye fillets, or whole smelt

Kosher salt and freshly ground pepper

½ medium fennel bulb, thinly sliced

1 leek, root end trimmed, thinly sliced crosswise

1 garlic clove, smashed and peeled

2 fresh bay leaves

½ cup white wine

¼ cup Begonia Vinegar (page 41)

¼ cup chopped roasted red peppers

2 tablespoons toasted pine nuts

2 teaspoons capers, chopped, with their brine

1 tablespoon golden raisins

1 tablespoon "gold standard" olive oil (see page 23)

Zest of 1 lemon

Everyone from the Spanish and Italians to the Greeks and Nordics (and even us Americans) have a tradition of eating fish that is fried one day and then packed in oil, vinegar, and vegetables to chow on the next. This widely shared recipe provides a way to stretch a particular fish into several future meals (back in the day, it was also a way to preserve food when there was no refrigeration). With this particular recipe, we call for fish "in saor" because, by Venetian standards, where this specific twist originates, we want an acidic and minimally sweet (aka sour) marinade for the fish. The idea here is that you pick a fish (it doesn't really matter what it is, but tradition would have you grab sardines, smelts, anchovies, herrings, or trout); chop it up into pieces that will fit into a jar; fry it all the way through; pack it into the jar; cover it with oil, vinegar, and vegetables; and store it. It'll be much less chewy than a pickled piece of fish but still delicious. And really, isn't that the point of something you'll be eating over and over again anyway?

1 In a large, heavy sauté pan over medium-high heat, warm the ½ cup grapeseed oil to 350°F on an instant-read thermometer. If your oil is smoking or too hot, just remove the pan from the heat and wait a minute or two. (Don't panic by throwing water into the pan or pouring the oil down the sink; you could severely hurt yourself or burn your house down.)

2 Place the flour into a shallow baking dish.

3 While the oil is heating, season the fish aggressively with salt and pepper, then dredge it in the flour. Be sure to shake off any excess flour from the fish.

4 Carefully place the fish in the hot oil and fry until golden brown on both sides, about 3 minutes per side. (At this point the fish will be cooked.) Remove the fish from the pan and place it in a shallow baking dish.

5 Discard the oil from the sauté pan and add the remaining 1 tablespoon grapeseed oil, the fennel, leek, garlic, and bay leaves and season with salt. Cover and cook over medium heat, stirring frequently, for 10 minutes. Then, add the wine and let reduce completely, about 5 minutes more. Add the vinegar and let it reduce by one-fourth; stir in the roasted peppers, pine nuts, capers, and raisins; and then immediately pour over the fish. Top with the olive oil and lemon zest, and let cool to room temperature before serving, or transfer to an airtight container and refrigerate for up to 1 week.

COLD-SMOKED SALMON
(AKA LOX)

Makes about 3½ pounds; serves 8

1 cup kosher salt

¾ cup sugar

5 tablespoons cracked coriander seeds

2 tablespoons cracked black peppercorns

2 tablespoons cracked juniper berries

2 tablespoons caraway seeds

1 bunch dill, stems and leaves chopped

¼ cup Old-School Red Wine Vinegar (page 34)

4 pounds king salmon fillets

A sprawling spread of lox, bagels, and cream cheese is a mainstay of many kitchen tables across the United States almost every day. Hell, *our* most productive days making this book typically started that way, with a smattering of incredible baked goods, schmears, and cured fish that were made in-house or provided by friends. Although making lox might seem intimidating for two reasons—first, it is part of the culinary backbone of perhaps America's greatest (and arguably snobbiest) food mecca, New York City; second, because of this association, lox also seems expensive— luckily for you, despite those stereotypes, this cured fish can be whipped up cheaply in your own kitchen. As Jadakiss, a member of the Yonkers, New York–based rap supergroup The LOX, once defiantly said, "We gonna make it." Toast up a bagel, slather it with a schmear, and top it all off with the salmon. Or enjoy it as a salad with some lettuce, vinaigrette, capers, and crispy shallots—you can't go wrong.

We use a dry brine for this recipe. While the word *dry* doesn't seem to jibe with the word *brine*, which many will automatically assume means something wet, this cure finds itself somewhere in between. It's a thick vinegary paste of salt and sugar that is liberally applied. We also recommend cold smoking this salmon. If you don't have a smoker, don't sweat it; the fish will be plenty delicious without the smoke.

1 In a large bowl, combine the salt, sugar, coriander, peppercorns, juniper berries, caraway seeds, and dill. Stir in the vinegar to make a brine. Gently rub one-fourth of the brine all over the fish.

2 Pour one-fourth of the remaining brine into a small, shallow pan. Place the salmon, skin-side down, on the brine and cover with the rest of the brine. Let the salmon marinate for at least 12 hours or up to 14 hours so the cure fully takes hold.

3 After curing, dip the fillets in a bowl of ice-cold water to rinse off any lingering brine. Let the fish rest, uncovered, in the refrigerator for 24 hours to dry out and to let the flavor of the brine equalize throughout the fillet. This will allow the smoke to better adhere to the fish.

4 Set up a smoker according to the manufacturer's instructions. Add the salmon and smoke at 80°F for 3 hours, then take a bite; the fish is properly smoked when it has a distinctly smoky flavor (don't worry so much hitting a certain temperature but don't smoke for longer than 6 hours). After the fish is smoked, transfer to a plate and refrigerate, covered, for at least 2 hours and up to 12 hours before serving. Store, tightly wrapped in plastic, in the refrigerator for up to 1 week, or, in ziplock bags, in the freezer for up to 6 months.

VARIATION You can also coat the fillets pastrami-style before smoking by topping them off with an additional mix of the coriander, peppercorns, caraway seeds, juniper berries, and dill.

TOFU JERKY

Makes 8 ounces; serves 4 as a snack

2 cups neutral oil

1 cup miso

1 cup Umami-Infused Vinegar (page 44)

½ cup Dijon mustard (see page 90)

3 tablespoons honey

2 tablespoons peeled and grated fresh ginger

2 tablespoon grated garlic

2 tablespoons black peppercorns

1 tablespoon red pepper flakes

Two 8-ounce packages soft tofu, drained of all water and sliced into ½-inch planks

I love beef jerky so much that I attempted the unthinkable—create a tofu iteration! What prompted my gonzo experiment? My wife, inadvertently. She's a vegetarian, and I wondered why she—someone who used to love meat as much as I do—couldn't enjoy this wonderful food just because of her dietary choices. We're not going to include the original version of the recipe because it involves koji, a wonderful but truly difficult-to-grow fungus for home cooks messing with it for the first time. This tofu recipe is simpler, and it can be used for everything from a vegan mapo tofu base to a vegan chili. It's the meatiest of the nonmeat excursions we've got in this book.

1   In a blender, combine the oil, miso, vinegar, mustard, honey, ginger, garlic, peppercorns, and red pepper flakes and puree to make an emulsified marinade. (Don't worry about adding the oil slowly for a proper emulsification; the amount of mustard and miso makes this sauce nearly "unbreakable.")

2   In a 9 by 9-inch baking pan, place the tofu in a single layer and then pour in the emulsified marinade. Refrigerate, covered, for at least 24 hours or up to 72 hours. If the marinade doesn't completely cover the tofu, flip the tofu halfway through the marinating process to ensure that it penetrates evenly.

3   After the tofu has marinated, preheat the oven to 170°F. Line a baking sheet with parchment paper or a silicone baking mat.

4   Remove the tofu from the marinade, place it on the prepared baking sheet, and dry in the oven until it has the texture of beef jerky, 8 to 12 hours; the longer it dries, the more jerky-like it becomes. Store in an airtight container, at room temperature, for up to 1 week or in the refrigerator for up to 3 weeks.

5 HOT VINEGAR-BASED SAUCES

(AKA PAN SAUCES)

Steak sauce. French sauce with wine. That tangy pasta condiment with clam juice, garlic, and Parmesan that your favorite restaurant makes. All of these condiments are bona fide vinaigrettes. However, what separates these acidic liquids from their chapter 3 cousins is heat. Once a vinaigrette hits the pan, it becomes a "pan sauce." Why? I don't know. We don't argue with the arbitrary jargon of our cheffing forefathers.

When it comes to pan sauces, I think, as a rule of thumb, we need to consider the unctuousness (aka the fat) alongside the level of acidity. Pan sauces that rely on lots of butter, foie gras, and animal drippings are going to see their acidity levels drop—therefore, you'll need lots of vinegar to even them out. On the other end, sauces that balance some garlic and pasta-cooking or vegetable-blanching water with a smidgen of bacon require only a little bit of vinegar. When it comes to teaching young cooks these rules, I make sure they know that pan sauces are never permanently broken. You're always a step or two away from emulsifying or re-emulsifying your vinaigrette.

One thing is for certain: Mixing up acidity with fat, salt, and sugar is how we cook great food. So let's kick it up a notch from cold sauces, roll up our sleeves, and dive into the mildly more difficult process of creating hot pan sauces.

HOLIDAY YAM SOUP, YEMENITE-STYLE

Serves 6

2 pounds turkey necks
or wings

4 tablespoons schmaltz

1 large yam or sweet
potato, grated, plus
1 medium yam or
sweet potato

1 cup grated yellow onion

1 cup grated carrot

½ cup cilantro, thinly
sliced all the way to the
stem ends

4 tablespoons
hawaij spice blend

Kosher salt and freshly
ground pepper

1 tablespoon Modernist
Cucumber Vinegar
(page 39)

8 cups water

2 tablespoons bread
crumbs (see page 27),
toasted

This is a favorite of the Sawyer family during the fall and winter. It's filling, comforting, and the perfect way to end a snowy winter day in Cleveland. I love the Yemenite spice mix *hawaij,* a sublime mix of cumin, black pepper, turmeric, and cardamom; it elevates this from good to great. After one spoonful, you'll be wondering why you haven't had this soup before.

1 Preheat the oven to 400°F.

2 Place the turkey necks or wings in a roasting pan and then roast until golden brown, 30 to 40 minutes.

3 Meanwhile, in large, heavy stockpot over medium heat, melt 2 tablespoons of the schmaltz. Add the grated yam, onion, carrot, cilantro, and 3 tablespoons of the hawaij spice blend and season with salt and pepper. Cover and sweat the veggies until thoroughly cooked, about 7 minutes. Then, add the vinegar and deglaze the pot, scraping up any browned bits with a wooden spoon.

4 Add the roasted turkey and water to the pot and stir to combine. Bring to a boil, then lower the heat to a simmer. Add the whole yam and simmer until the yam is cooked through, about 25 minutes.

5 Remove the yam from the pot and let cool to room temperature, then peel, cut it in half lengthwise, and slice into 1-inch-thick half-moons. In a small bowl, toss the yam slices with the remaining 2 tablespoons schmaltz and season with salt and pepper. Set aside while the soup finishes.

6 Simmer the soup for 1 hour more, then remove and discard the turkey necks. Using an immersion blender, blend the soup to a smooth consistency.

7 Place some yam slices in each soup bowl, ladle in some soup, and sprinkle with the bread crumbs and remaining 1 tablespoon hawaij spice. Serve immediately.

CHICKPEA AND TOMATO LEBRON (NOT STEPH) CURRY

Serving 6

2 tablespoons
coconut oil

2 tablespoons ghee

1 medium onion, peeled
and small diced

1 medium carrot, peeled
and small diced

1 bunch cilantro,
stems and leaves,
thinly sliced and
kept separate

3 garlic cloves, minced

2 teaspoons
tomato paste

¼ cup curry paste

3 cups cooked chickpeas

2 curry, lime, or bay
leaves (whatever you
can find, dried or fresh)

2 tablespoons
Umami-Infused Vinegar
(page 44) or white wine
vinegar (see variation,
page 34)

1 tablespoon
vadouvan spice

2 cups peeled, diced,
and strained tomatoes

3 to 10 Thai bird chiles,
thinly sliced (adjust for
your level of heat)

1 cup chicken stock
or water

1 tablespoon kosher salt

3 cups Proper Rice Pilaf
(facing page)

Zest of 1 lime

⅓ cup plain yogurt

6 pieces pappadam
or naan

As a native Clevelander, I'm a die-hard fan of the city's NBA team, the Cavaliers, and its (as of this writing) superstar player, Akron native LeBron James. Besides the numerous personal accolades he's stacked up over the course of his career, he brought Cleveland the championship in 2016 (the city's first in 52 years) and he has given back to the community and northeast Ohio at large, in numerous ways. He's a true Ohioan and one of the best representatives we've got. Therefore, I feel it's only right that I name a recipe in this book after The King—and at the joking expense of a rival, Akron-born Steph Curry.

So, curry—why's it in here? Well, like mole and ragù Bolognese, curry contains multitudes of influences and showcases glorious differences depending upon who's making it; and the opportunity to personalize the recipe is here for the taking. I love dining at a restaurant that asks if you want it *hot*, giving you the ability to customize its heat on a 1-to-5 scale. If you answer 5, then they'll ask if you want "hot" or "Indian hot." And if you're seeking spice, then it's necessary to consume a pile of rice pilaf to temper the Scovilles. In the grand scheme of things, rice pilaf is rarely venerated. Sure, risotto and sushi rice get their due, but I think cafeterias and buffets that have pilaf get a bad rap. The pilaf recipe makes more than you will need for the curry; one of my favorite kitchen snacks is pilaf with some hot sauce and butter. The curry will keep in an airtight container, refrigerated, for up to 3 days.

1   In a large pot over medium heat, melt the coconut oil and ghee. Add the onion, carrot, and cilantro stems and cook, stirring occasionally, for 7 minutes, until the onion has softened. Add the garlic, tomato paste, and curry paste; turn the heat to high; and cook, stirring occasionally, for 7 minutes more, until the tomato and curry pastes have darkened considerably.

2   Add the chickpeas, curry leaves, vinegar, and 1 teaspoon of the vadouvan to the pot and deglaze, using a wooden spoon to scrape up any bits that have stuck to the pot's bottom. Add the tomatoes, chiles, chicken stock, and salt and stir to combine. Turn the heat to medium-high, cover the pot, and let simmer for 10 minutes.

3   Place a scoop of the rice pilaf on each dinner plate, top with the curry, and garnish with the lime zest, yogurt, cilantro leaves, and remaining 2 teaspoons vadouvan. Serve immediately, with the pappadam on the side.

PROPER RICE PILAF *Makes about 6 cups*

2 cups long-grain
basmati rice

1 tablespoon "gold
standard" olive oil
(see page 23)

1 shallot, minced

1 teaspoon kosher salt

4 cups chicken stock

2 tablespoons
salted butter

2 garlic cloves

2 bay leaves

1 dried morel or shiitake
mushroom

1 Place the rice in a large bowl, cover
with 6 cups cold water, and let soak
for 20 to 60 minutes.

2 Preheat the oven to 350°F.

3 In an ovenproof, lidded pot over
medium heat, warm the olive oil.
Add the shallot and salt and sauté
for 5 minutes. Drain the rice and
then add it to the pot, toasting for
2 minutes and stirring constantly.
Add the chicken stock, butter,
garlic, bay leaves, and mushroom;
cover; and place the pot in the oven
to cook for 12 to 15 minutes.

4 Remove the pot from the oven, stir
and fluff the rice with a fork, and
then allow to cool for a couple of
minutes, partially covered, before
serving. Or, transfer to an airtight
container and store, refrigerated,
for up to 2 days.

WHOLE TURNIPS APICIUS WITH GARLIC GARAM VINEGAR, GOLDEN RAISINS, FENNEL SEED & KHLEA

Serves 2

1 pound Tokyo turnips or any small sweet turnips, including greens

2 tablespoons Khlea (facing page)

2 tablespoons salted butter

1 teaspoon to 1 tablespoon Garlic Garum Vinegar (facing page)

½ cup golden raisins

1 teaspoon cracked fennel seeds

Kosher salt

Zest of 1 lemon

1 tablespoon bread crumbs (see page 27)

The fourth- or fifth-century book commonly known as *Apicius* is a must-read for all cooks, Italians, Romans, historians, nerds, and foodies alike. It is generally credited as the first written cookbook, and the work features recipes for peacock, fermented wheat (soy sauce, sort of), garum (fish sauce), balut egg (fetal egg shots), and much more. In order to truly get the most out of this recipe, which pays homage to the OG recipes you'll find in *Apicius*, ask your local butcher for aged beef fat; if they don't have any, ask for duck fat. Have them double-grind the beef fat very fine; in the case of the duck fat, it will already be rendered, so you can skip that step. I have a jar of rendered fat that has been passed down from my mom and my mom's mom; I add any nonpork fats into it whenever I cook at home—it lasts forever and gets weirder every year we age it. If you prefer, you can simply substitute duck fat or schmaltz (rendered poultry fat) here. This recipe provides enough khlea to make this dish several times over.

Our own garlic garum vinegar ferments in an oak barrel for at least three months, so I highly recommend making a double or even triple batch and aging it in an old wine bottle or small wooden barrel. It will never spoil and gets better with age.

1 Remove and wash the turnip greens and thinly slice them crosswise.

2 In a sauté pan over medium heat, combine the khlea and butter. Add the turnips and let them brown a little and start to caramelize, about 10 minutes. Add the turnip greens and a splash of water to steam them; the greens will be wilted within a minute. Add the vinegar to your liking (1 teaspoon for beginners or 1 tablespoon if you're feeling like a crazy Roman infantryman).

3 Stir the raisins and fennel seeds into the turnips and season with salt. Transfer the mixture to a bowl and garnish with the lemon zest and bread crumbs. Serve immediately.

KHLEA *Makes about 4 ounces*

2 quarts water

6 ounces aged raw beef fat, double-ground

In a large stockpot over low heat, combine the water and beef fat and let simmer until all the water has evaporated and only the fat remains, about 20 minutes. Carefully strain the fat into an airtight glass container; discarding the solids. Store, refrigerated, indefinitely.

GARLIC GARUM VINEGAR *Makes about 1 pint*

4 garlic cloves

1 cup fish sauce (preferably Red Boat)

1 cup Greenhouse Tavern–Style Craft-Beer Vinegar (page 32)

1 On a cutting board and using the back of a knife, crush the garlic to release the juices. In a mason jar, combine the crushed garlic and its juices, the fish sauce, and vinegar.

2 Cover the jar securely with a piece of cheesecloth and let the mixture ferment, at room temperature, for 1 week before using. The vinegar will keep, covered, at room temperature, indefinitely.

ARTICHOKES À LA GRECQUE

Serves 2 to 4

1 gallon cold water,
plus more as needed

1 cup distilled vinegar

4 tablespoons
kosher salt

8 artichokes

½ lemon, plus flesh
of 1 lemon, quartered
(pith and skin should be
peeled and discarded)

4 tablespoons neutral oil

1 fennel bulb,
sliced crosswise into
¼-inch rings

1 onion, sliced crosswise
into ¼-inch rings

1 small celery heart,
sliced

3 fresh bay leaves

2 cups white wine
(preferably Chablis or
Chardonnay)

4 tablespoons salted
cultured butter

1 bunch thyme,
leaves picked

1 cup white wine vinegar
(see variation, page 34)

I came about this recipe a super-long time ago as a young culinarian. I think when you're creative, you tend to break traditions. I didn't understand why artichokes were made only two ways: peeled and poached, or steamed whole and enjoyed one leaf at a time. I just thought the process was flawed. It didn't make sense to me.

One of the first things I did while in culinary school was explore the artichoke family. I found cardoons, a close relative to the artichoke, and then their sunflower cousins, and I made as many different dishes with them as I could find recipes for. I was furthering my research. One of the next things I did was to infuse all the trimmings from the cardoons and sunflowers with butter over low heat. That moment is what spurred me to think, *Okay, it's not that bitter. There has to be a better way to eliminate the bitterness.* For artichokes, I figured out the same thing, settling on a purging technique that correlated with a really old recipe, utilizing freezing-cold water and super-high levels of both vinegar and lemon juice. Now, I incorporate a hot-water rinse to remove the cynarine (the acid responsible the bitter taste) out of the base of the artichoke. Finally, I poach the artichoke in a broth heavy with white wine vinegar and lemon. The result is an artichoke broth that can be used to build a soup or sauce or to poach fish. It's the most amazing flavor that restaurants don't use very often. And people are usually like, *Holy shit, I can't believe you can do that.* They usually associate artichokes with goopy sauces like mayo, aioli, or hollandaise. So I've included this recipe to help expand your mind on the versatility of the mighty artichoke. The artichokes and garnishes are used in Sustainable Fish in Cartoccio with Wild Mushrooms, Artichokes à la Grecque, New Potato & Meyer Lemon (page 179) but can also be eaten on their own. Use them as you would canned artichoke hearts; they're great mixed with olives, tossed into a salad, or made into a filling for ravioli.

For this recipe, you'll need a couple types of knives: a serrated knife and a stainless-steel paring knife or tourné knife (which is similar to a paring knife but has a curved blade).

CONTINUED

1   In a large bowl, combine the water, distilled vinegar, and 3 tablespoons of the salt, stirring to dissolve the salt. Set aside.

2   Using a serrated knife, slice one artichoke from the top of the choke to just above the heart (i.e., the light green area of flesh; the heart starts at the bottom of the artichoke and, measuring toward the top, is about 1 inch thick). Place the artichoke on a cutting board so that the top of the choke faces you. With the serrated knife, trim the tough green outer leaves surrounding the heart to the lighter yellow-green core. Aggressively rub the entire artichoke with the lemon half so it doesn't oxidize and turn brown; discard all the leaves and trim.

3   Using a paring knife, peel and trim the artichoke from heart to stem, turning the artichoke and trimming and cutting all the way to the yellow core. Rub again with the lemon half. Place the artichoke, heart-side down, on the cutting board and then slice off almost half of the artichoke from just past the stem. Use the paring knife to cut the pieces of thistle out of the resulting artichoke pieces. You cannot stop the peeling process once you start; if you do, the artichokes will oxidize amazingly fast—you definitely don't want this to happen. However, if you have to

stop, submerge the artichokes in the vinegar-salt water to prevent them from oxidizing. The key to success is working quickly and cleanly. Peel and trim the remaining artichokes in the same manner, soaking them in the vinegar-salt water for 30 to 90 minutes, at room temperature, before proceeding.

4   Rinse each artichoke under hot water for a couple of minutes prior to cooking. This purges the artichoke of most of its cynarine.

5   In a large lidded stockpot over medium heat, combine the oil, fennel, onion, celery heart, and bay leaves and season with the remaining 1 tablespoon salt, stirring to dissolve the salt. Cover and cook until the vegetables look translucent, 5 to 15 minutes; make sure you're sweating and not caramelizing the mixture. Then, add the wine, butter, thyme, and lemon flesh and boil for 5 minutes. Add the artichokes and white wine vinegar and water to cover.

6   Place the lid on the stockpot and poach the artichokes over medium heat until they are cooked through and fork-tender, about 20 minutes. Remove from the heat and let cool to room temperature, then refrigerate, covered, for up to 1 week.

RATATOUILLE NICOISE

Serves 4

1 small Thai eggplant
(see Note), halved
lengthwise

5 Padrón or shishito
peppers

1 small yellow squash,
halved lengthwise

1 small zucchini, halved
lengthwise

20 cherry tomatoes

1 cup fresh herbes de
Provence (see Note)

¼ cup Old-School Red
Wine Vinegar (page 34)

¼ cup "gold standard"
olive oil (see page 23),
plus more for drizzling

Kosher salt and freshly
ground pepper

2 cups brodo
(see page 115)

1 small yellow onion,
brûléed (see Note)

1 cup tomato passato
(see Note)

2 tablespoons salted
cultured butter

¼ cup Nicoise olives

10 squash blossoms

4 ounces Banon
goat cheese

¼ cup bread crumbs
(see page 27)

We can thank a famous animated French rodent for breathing fresh life into this rustic peasant vegetable dish from Provence. But long before chef Thomas Keller's Disney-fied version came along, ratatouille was just an herb stew that featured zucchini, squash, tomato, and eggplant. Ratatouille adheres to the mantra that if it grows together, then it belongs together. However, don't be fooled by the simplicity of this recipe. It's a total showstopper that's elevated by the quality of its components—make sure you source high-quality local ingredients—and a proper cooking technique.

1 Preheat the grill to medium-high.

2 In a large bowl, combine the eggplant, Padróns, squash, zucchini, 15 cherry tomatoes, ½ cup of the herbes de Provence, ⅛ cup of the vinegar, and the olive oil and season with salt and pepper. Using your hands, mix everything together.

3 Transfer the vegetables to the grill and cook until just warmed up; about 10 minutes for the zucchini, squash, and eggplant, and just 5 minutes for the Padróns and tomatoes. Using tongs, remove the vegetables from the grill when they are ready.

4 In a large, heavy saucepan over medium heat, combine the brodo, onion, tomato passato, remaining 5 cherry tomatoes, and 2 tablespoons herbes de Provence. Cook, stirring occasionally to prevent sticking, until highly aromatic, about 15 minutes.

5 Carefully place the tomato mixture in a blender, add the butter and remaining ⅛ cup vinegar, and blend until smooth.

6 Return the blended tomato mixture to the saucepan. Add all the grilled vegetables, the olives, squash blossoms, and remaining herbes de Provence. Stir to combine and then let the mixture rest, off the heat, for 10 minutes.

7 Spread goat cheese in the bottom of four pasta bowls and then pour the vegetable mixture on top. Garnish each dish with bread crumbs and a drizzle of olive oil. Serve immediately.

NOTES You can substitute any eggplant variety for Thai eggplants; just be sure to cut larger ones into the same size pieces as the squash and zucchini.

Fresh herbes de Provence are a combination of bush basil, thyme, rosemary, lavender, and parsley.

To make yellow onion brûlée, follow the procedure for Red Onion Brûlée on page 173, using 1 small yellow onion, 1 teaspoon olive oil, and a pinch of salt.

Passato is passed tomato or tomato sauce with just tomato, salt, and extra-virgin olive oil as ingredients.

PASTA AGLIO E OLIO CON PEPERONCINO

Serves 2

1 pound spaghetti

3 tablespoons "gold standard" olive oil (see page 23)

3 garlic cloves, peeled and thinly sliced

1 tablespoon crushed dried arbol chile

1 teaspoon white wine vinegar (see variation, page 34)

1 tablespoon unsalted butter

2 tablespoons grated salty aged pecorino (such as Moliterno)

1 teaspoon fish sauce

Kosher salt

2 tablespoons bread crumbs (see page 27)

Attention all young and/or single people! You need to commit this pasta recipe to memory. Why? Several reasons. First, it's a can't-fail meal to execute when you're trying to woo a boo thang at home. Second, all of the partiers in your life—yourself included—will love devouring this pan-sauce classic before they sleep off their drunk (just don't burn the place down, okay?). And third, pasta aficionados will go bonkers for this cheese-chile-fish-sauce-drenched spaghetti dish.

Trust me, I've used Pasta Aglio e Olio con Peperoncino for all three reasons. Typically, our household pantry always contains the ingredients, so I can whip it up at a second's notice. Therefore, no matter what time it is or whom I'm with, this pasta can appear. Need further convincing about its power? In Italy, it's pretty much law that every person knows how to make it. In most Italian households, it's not even a recipe—it's an improvisation. Set your mind free and knock yourself out.

1 Bring a large pot of salted water to a boil. Add the pasta and cook until al dente, per the manufacturer's instructions.

2 While the pasta is cooking, in a large sauté pan over low heat, combine half of the olive oil, the garlic, and one-fourth of the chile and gently fry to brown the garlic.

3 Barely drain the cooked pasta, leaving some water clinging to the noodles (this will help emulsify the pan sauce). Add the pasta and vinegar to the sauté pan, turn the heat to medium-high, and add half of the remaining chile. Once the water begins to evaporate, turn off the heat and add the remaining oil, the butter, half of the pecorino, and the fish sauce. Stir vigorously, then taste and add salt if needed.

4 Divide the pasta among two bowls and garnish with the bread crumbs and remaining chile and pecorino. Serve immediately.

NOTE To take this dish to the next level, replace the olive oil with equal measurements of schmaltz (rendered poultry fat) or aged beef suet. I would also go super soigné and hit the sauce with a thyme sprig or bay leaf while it cooks.

STEAK FRITES WITH RED WINE VINEGAR DEMI-GLACE BEURRE

Serves 2

Two 8-ounce bistro steaks, trimmed; trim reserved and diced

Kosher salt and freshly ground pepper

3 cups Côtes du Rhône red wine

1 cup Old-School Red Wine Vinegar (page 34)

1 cup rich dark stock, demi-glace, or roasted beef or chicken stock that has been reduced by half

1 medium shallot, minced

1 fresh bay leaf

1 tablespoon unsalted butter

1 recipe The Greenhouse Tavern's Proper Pommes Frites (page 81)

When it comes to this recipe, I need to share with you two unrelated things—the first being why I'm obsessed with demi-glace, the rich, brown French sauce.

I love a classic, sticky veal demi-glace, but I don't love buying bones specifically to make it. We prefer to use the bones of the animals we are butchering and eating. This recipe is the ultimate demi-glace go-to for home cooks, utilizing trim and waste from the steaks to fortify the sauce. Tougher, tastier belly cuts, like skirt, flank, hanger, or shell, or a shoulder cut, like tri-tip, flat iron, or chuck roll, have traditionally been the favorite of chefs in France, thus the moniker "bistro steak." Pair this demi-glace with the Greenhouse Tavern's Proper Pommes Frites and a fat glass of Rhône red, and all will be bliss.

Now that we've got that out of the way, let this anecdote about my hero, friend, and spirit animal, chef Jonathan Waxman, inspire you to create this next-level pairing. So, Jonathan was a bit of a man-about-town in 1980s NYC with numerous legendary stories from the era. My favorite is when he hopped on a Concorde for Paris shortly after breakfast one Tuesday. When the owners of Jams (Jonathan's original California-inspired NYC joint) went looking for him as dinner service began, Jonathan suddenly strolled in the front door looking well fed and as posh as ever. When they asked, "Where were you?" Jonathan casually replied, "I was eating steak frites. . . ." But before his true whereabouts registered with management, Jonathan bluntly told them, "in Paris."

Now do like Jonathan and slam some out-of-this-world steak frites and demi-glace.

1 Season the steaks with salt and pepper and allow them to sit at room temperature for at least 1 hour and up to 4 hours before cooking.

2 In a large cast-iron skillet over medium-high heat, render the steak trim with a few tablespoons of water, stirring frequently, until almost burnt, about 20 minutes. Remove the skillet from the heat and allow it to cool to room

CONTINUED

temperature. Strain and reserve all the beef fat. Transfer all the browned beef trim to a large stainless-steel saucepan and cover with the wine and ¾ cup of the vinegar.

3 Set the saucepan over medium-high heat, reduce the liquid by half, then add the stock, shallot, and bay leaf. Bring the mixture to a boil, then turn the heat to low and position your pan on the burner so it simmers just on one side of the pan. Reduce the liquid by three-fourths, 1 to 2 hours, skimming off the impurities that bubble to the surface. Strain and transfer the sauce to a small saucepan, stir in the remaining ¼ cup vinegar, and set over low heat to keep warm.

4 Place the cast-iron skillet in the oven (no need to wipe the skillet clean) and preheat to 500°F.

5 When the oven is fully heated, carefully remove the pan and set it on a burner over high heat. Add 1 tablespoon of the rendered beef fat and the steaks and sear. Once the first sides are brown, about 3 minutes, flip each steak, add another 1 tablespoon rendered fat, place the skillet in the oven, and cook the steak to your desired doneness; for a big bistro steak, the total cooking time is less than 10 minutes for medium. Let the steaks rest for 5 minutes.

6 Return to the warm sauce and whisk in the butter, a little bit at a time, to achieve a fully emulsified sauce.

7 Slice the steaks as desired, dress with the sauce, and plate them with the pommes frites. Serve immediately.

CRISPY OHIO PORK (NOT) BELLY

Serves 4 to 6

3 pounds boneless pork shoulder

2 tablespoons Muscovado sugar

1 tablespoon high-quality unrefined sea salt (preferably Redmond's Real Salt)

1 tablespoon red pepper flakes

2 quarts Cream Soda Vinegar (page 40)

10 cipollini or pearl onions, peeled

Kosher salt and freshly ground black pepper

2 tablespoons salted butter

½ pound chanterelle or chicken of the woods mushrooms

½ pound oyster mushrooms

1 tablespoon fresh lemon thyme leaves

Any breathing, sentient human within the last ten years has encountered the unfortunate "bacon everything" fad. People used bacon for such disparate items as waffle cones and garnishing for smoked-whiskey cocktails. It was gross. Because of it, we refused to feature pork belly as an item. But one day an idea came to us: If the people demand pork belly, then screw it, we'll give it to them . . . kind of.

Being the counterculture aficionado that I am, it seemed only appropriate to use some cheeky verbiage to get people to order pork that's not belly or bacon—that is, the shoulder and cheek, which are close enough muscle-, fat-, and flavor-wise to beloved bacon. For us, they're essentially interchangeable. We like to cook our pork low and slow, so we do a combination technique of steaming and roasting on a resting rack covered with foil in a deep roasting pan; the vinegar provides our steam, which helps break down the texture of the pork and imparts a beautiful aroma. No dish exemplifies our love of local pork better than this one; we recommend using your trusted local butcher for sourcing the pork and tying it for cooking. The recipe name says it all—and you can't call us biters for doing it.

This dish is fairly time intensive. It takes shape over the course of three days. I love starting it on Thursday night and enjoying for Sunday dinner.

1 Rub the pork with the sugar, sea salt, and red pepper flakes. Wrap it tightly in plastic and let cure in the refrigerator overnight.

2 The next day, preheat the oven to 300°F. Set a resting rack in a roasting pan.

3 Place the pork on the prepared rack and pour the vinegar into the bottom of the roasting pan. Cover tightly with aluminum foil, place in the oven, and steam the pork for 4 hours. Remove and uncover the pork; pour the steaming liquid into a container to save for finishing the dish and then refrigerate.

CONTINUED

4 Turn the oven temperature to 400°F.

5 Return the pork to the oven, uncovered, and roast until it has a crispy golden top, about 20 minutes. Remove the pork from the oven and let cool to room temperature. Remove the pork from the pan, wrap it tightly in plastic wrap, and place in baking dish. Set a weight, such as a couple of large cans, on top of the pork and let rest in the refrigerator overnight. This helps all the individual muscles that make up this cut of meat stay together.

6 The next day, in a large saucepan over medium heat, bring the reserved pork-steaming liquid to a simmer. Add the onions and poach them until cooked through, about 20 minutes. Strain the onions, reserving the poaching liquid.

7 While the onions poach, unwrap the pork and cut it into 2-inch-thick steaks. Season lightly with kosher salt and black pepper.

8 In a sauté pan over medium-high heat, melt 1 tablespoon of the butter. Add the pork and poached onions and sear on one side until fully caramelized, or deep golden brown, about 5 minutes. Remove everything from the pan, place onto a large serving platter, and let rest for 2 minutes.

9 In the same pan over medium-high heat, melt the remaining 1 table-spoon butter. Add all the mushrooms, season with kosher salt and black pepper, and sauté to a light golden brown, about 7 minutes. Remove the mushrooms from the pan and place them on top of the pork and onions.

10 Add about 2 cups of the reserved poaching liquid to the pan and deglaze, scraping up any browned bits with a wooden spoon. Then, add the thyme and simmer for a few minutes to reduce by a third. Pour the sauce over the pork, onions, and mushrooms. Serve immediately.

FOIE GRAS–STEAMED CLAMS

Serves 1 or 2

12 middleneck clams

¼ cup water, plus more as needed

2 tablespoons Red Onion Brûlée (facing page)

1 tablespoon unsalted butter, plus 1 teaspoon

1 tablespoon Foie Gras Butter (facing page)

2 teaspoons Greenhouse Tavern–Style Craft-Beer Vinegar (page 32)

Kosher salt

Grilled slices of crusty sourdough bread for serving

When I worked for Charlie Palmer at Kitchen 22 in NYC, we once found ourselves with an abundance of slow cookers after hosting an event. Despite feeling absolutely blessed that we stumbled ass-backward into these free devices, Charlie forced us to use them in everyday service. Friend and, later on, Greenhouse Tavern chef Brian Goodman and I, as extremely young and naive cooks, decided to add foie gras to everything we prepared in these slow cookers—heck, we even threw some in our coffee. We didn't care. So one day, Brian turns to me and jokingly says, "Why not finish a clam dish with foie gras instead of butter?" I then added to the gastronomical anarchy by suggesting, "Why don't we just mount a foie gras mousse in the clams instead of butter?" Voilà, the Greenhouse Tavern's famous foie gras–steamed clams were born.

1 In a medium sauté pan over high heat, combine the clams, water, red onion brûlée, 1 tablespoon unsalted butter, and 1 teaspoon of the foie gras butter. Cover and cook until the clams pop open, 3 to 4 minutes; discard any clams that don't open. The pan sauce will be broken; you'll notice that the fat and liquid have separated. Once the clams are open, use tongs to transfer them to a serving vessel to prevent overcooking.

2 Turn off the heat and, whisking constantly, emulsify the steaming liquid with the remaining 2 teaspoons foie gras butter, remaining 1 teaspoon unsalted butter, and the vinegar. If the sauce begins to break and separate, add more water, 1 teaspoon at a time, to re-emulsify. Taste and season with salt, if needed.

3 Pour the sauce over the clams and serve with a few pieces of grilled bread to sop up all of the sauce.

RED ONION BRÛLÉE *Makes about 5 tablespoons*

1 medium red onion, halved

1 tablespoon "silver standard" olive oil (see page 23)

1 teaspoon kosher salt

1. Preheat the oven to 300°F.

2. In a medium bowl, dress the onion halves with the olive oil and salt.

3. Place the onion, cut-side down, on a baking sheet, and roast until the skin pops off easily and the cut side of the onion is caramelized, 1½ to 2 hours. Remove and discard all the onion skin, then small-dice the flesh. Store in an airtight container, refrigerated, for up to 1 week.

FOIE GRAS BUTTER *Makes about 4 tablespoons*

2 tablespoons diced foie gras scraps

1 small yellow onion, julienned

2 tablespoons unsalted butter, at room temperature

Kosher salt

1. In a cast-iron skillet over high heat, sear the foie gras scraps (don't add any oil to the skillet; the foie will leak out plenty of fat) until caramelized, it should take on a rich, dark brown color, about 2 minutes. Remove the foie gras from pan and set aside to cool completely.

2. Add the onion to the skillet and cook in the rendered fat until caramelized, about 5 minutes. Remove the skillet from the heat, and let the onion cool in the fat.

3. In a food processor, combine the cooled foie, onion, and fat and process until it is almost smooth.

4. In the bowl of a stand mixer fitted with the paddle attachment, whip the butter and foie puree until evenly incorporated, then season with salt. Store in an airtight container, refrigerated, for up to 1 week, or in the freezer for up to 3 months. Let soften at room temperature for about 1 hour before using.

WALLEYE PIKE QUENELLES WITH TOMATOES

Serves 4 to 6

GRILLED OUT-OF-SEASON TOMATO SAUCE

8 Roma tomatoes (as ripe as can be expected out of season), halved

1 small yellow onion, halved

1 tablespoon "silver standard" olive oil (see page 23)

Kosher salt and freshly ground pepper

2 tablespoons unsalted butter

1 tablespoon Old-School Red Wine Vinegar (page 34)

QUENELLES

2¼ pounds walleye pike, perch, bass, or other white freshwater fish fillets

½ cup heavy cream

1 teaspoon fish sauce

1 cup water, plus 1 gallon

¾ cup unsalted butter, plus 2 tablespoons

Kosher salt

1 cup all-purpose flour

2 eggs, plus 4 egg yolks

One of my absolute favorite food memories from France is that of Pierre Gaillard's wife making freshwater pike quenelles. For more than forty years, the Gaillard family has been producing regal Côte-Rôtie and Condrieu wines on the sun-soaked slopes along the Rhône river at angles that are treacherous even by mountain-goat standards, yet the wines they yield are soft, subtle, supple, and velvety wonders. The risk is worth it for the reward.

During this particular trip, Pierre's wife procured the fish for the quenelles in one of the most badass ways I've ever heard. When she went down to the river, she spotted the pike's beady eyes poking out from the water and, in one fell swoop, snatched the fish and plopped it into her other hand, butchering it right then. Back in the kitchen, she turned it into a fine mousse and combined it with some milky white pâte à choux she pulled from the fridge. Then, she whipped out the quenelle spoons to form it into the three-ish-sided football that is the characteristic shape. It was incredible.

Here's my homage to those incredible quenelles. Like the Red Wine Vinegar Soubise on page 109, this tomato sauce is naturally onion-sweet and tastes balanced at every temperature. I would recommend using it as a sauce for any protein, but not on your pasta or pizza.

1 To make the tomato sauce: Preheat the grill to high.

2 In a large bowl, combine the tomatoes, onion, and olive oil; toss to mix; and season aggressively with salt and pepper.

3 Put the vegetables on the grill and let them develop an intense char on one side, about 7 minutes. Remove from the heat and let cool, then cut them into ¼-inch slices.

4 In a sauté pan over medium heat, melt the butter. Add the charred tomatoes and onion and cook, stirring frequently, until they soften and start to break down, about 30 minutes. Then, transfer the mixture to a food processor, add the vinegar, and carefully puree. Set aside and let cool.

CONTINUED

5   To make the quenelles: Using a fillet knife, clean the fish of its skin, blood line (the length of blood-rich muscle that runs parallel to the spine and situated right under the skin; it can be very strongly flavored and take on an unappealing color when cooked), and any blemishes.

6   In a food processor, combine the flesh, heavy cream, and fish sauce and puree until smooth. Remove the fish mousse from the processor and set aside in the refrigerator.

7   In a medium saucepan over medium-low heat, combine the 1 cup water, ¾ cup butter, and 2 teaspoons salt and quickly bring to a boil. Stirring constantly, sift in the flour, then turn the heat to medium and cook until the mixture begins pulling away from the sides of the pan. Continue to cook for 3 minutes more, allowing some evaporation to occur.

8   Transfer the warm mixture to the bowl of a stand mixer fitted with the paddle attachment. On medium speed, slowly incorporate the eggs and egg yolks, one at a time. Transfer the resulting pâte à choux to a bowl, cover with plastic wrap, and let cool in the refrigerator for 1 hour.

9   Once the choux is cool, fold in the fish mousse to form a batter.

10 In a large stockpot, bring the 1 gallon water to a simmer, season with salt, and then add the batter to the water, a spoonful at a time. Slowly poach the quenelles until they float to the surface, 4 to 6 minutes.

11 Meanwhile, in a medium sauté pan over medium-low heat, melt the remaining 2 tablespoons butter.

12 Once poached, transfer the cooked quenelles to the sauté pan and toss to coat with the butter. Top the quenelles with the reserved tomato sauce and allow guests to serve themselves from the pan.

SUSTAINABLE FISH IN CARTOCCIO WITH WILD MUSHROOMS, ARTICHOKES À LA GRECQUE, NEW POTATO & MEYER LEMON

Serves 2

2 Yukon gold potatoes, peeled, poached, and sliced 1 inch thick

4 dried morel or black trumpet mushrooms, diced

1 tablespoon "gold standard" olive oil (see page 23), plus more for drizzling

1 tablespoon lemon thyme leaves

Kosher salt

Two 5-ounce wild-caught halibut fillets (make sure it's sustainably harvested and skinless)

8 pieces Artichokes à la Grecque (page 159), plus ½ cup cooking liquid

4 tablespoons unsalted cultured butter

½ cup Chablis, white Burgundy, or Chardonnay wine

1 small Meyer lemon, thinly sliced

1 tablespoon bread crumbs (see page 27)

Fleur de sel

This dish is a great demo for home cooks. It was on our opening menu at the Greenhouse Tavern, at Trentina, and every Feast of the Seven Fishes holiday party at the Sawyer house. It's a classic technique that is foolproof for cooking fish at home. And, even better for you Instagram users, the presentation behind it is unrivaled. But know that grabbing a killer cut of fish is necessary for getting the most out of this recipe.

All of these steps can be done a day or two in advance. Most important, keep in mind that artichokes and wild mushrooms do not have to be the accoutrement you use *en papier*. You can also use any combination of ingredients—black truffle and celery, or dried tomato and olive, or Moroccan *merguez* sausage and caramelized onions. All are dope things to use in your final dish.

1 Preheat the oven to 350°F.

2 In a bowl, combine the potatoes, mushrooms, olive oil, and lemon thyme; season with kosher salt; and mix together with your hands.

3 Season the fish with kosher salt.

4 Place a 12-inch square of parchment paper in a baking dish. Center half of the potato mixture on the parchment, then layer on one fish fillet, half of the artichokes, 2 tablespoons of the butter, ¼ cup of the wine, and ¼ cup of the artichoke cooking liquid. Top with the lemon slices, then fold all the edges of the parchment square over themselves to seal the package. Repeat with a second square of parchment and the remaining ingredients.

5 Bake the fish until just cooked through, 10 to 15 minutes. (You'll know the fish is cooked through when you see the broth visibly bubbling from the bottom of the package just under the potato.)

6 Transfer the packages to two serving plates and let rest for a minute before serving. Once opened, anoint each with olive oil, bread crumbs, and fleur de sel.

FISH WITH BEGONIA VINEGAR

Serves 3

2 large red beets,
tops removed

Kosher salt

1 tablespoon
diced bacon

15 ounces sole, flounder,
fluke, or any other West
Coast rockfish, cut into
5-ounce portions

¼ cup plus
2 tablespoons blended
oil (see page 22)

2 teaspoons
unsalted butter

3 French Breakfast
radishes, tops removed,
quartered

3 ounces mustard
greens, cut crosswise
into 1-inch strips

½ cup brodo
(see page 115)

1 teaspoon Begonia
Vinegar (page 41)

1 teaspoon poppy seeds

1 teaspoon freshly
grated horseradish

1 large fresh mint leaf,
torn

This dish is inspired by Alain Passard, the vegetable wizard of L'Arpège fame (his graphic-novel cookbook is a revelation; I highly recommend it). Besides having one of the softest touches in the game, Passard is famous for putting monochromatic colors together on a plate, like white on white on white (white asparagus, endive, and salsify) and red on red on red on red (beets, lobster, saffron, and red carrot). It's a very interesting idea and yields delicious results. This sexy and simple recipe will not only taste incredible but also look Michelin-quality. It'll make you seem like you are a culinarian with multiple stars under your belt.

1   Preheat the oven to 350°F. Line a baking sheet with parchment paper.

2   Rinse the beets under cold running water and then toss with salt to season. Place the beets on the prepared baking sheet and roast until fork-tender, about 1 hour. Let cool, then peel the beets and cut into a medium dice.

3   While the beets are roasting, in a small skillet over medium heat, cook the bacon until crispy. Reserve it for garnish and discard the rendered fat.

4   Season the fish with salt.

5   Turn the oven temperature to 400°F. Place a large ovenproof sauté pan over high heat and a second large sauté pan over medium heat.

6   In the ovenproof sauté pan, warm the oil.

7   In the second pan, melt 1 teaspoon of the butter while taking care not to brown it. Add the quartered radishes, cook for 3 to 4 minutes, and then add the beets and mustard greens and sauté for another 3 minutes. Remove the vegetables from the pan and keep warm.

8   Add the brodo and vinegar to the pan and then the poppy seeds and remaining 1 teaspoon butter, whisking continuously to emulsify. Once the sauce is emulsified, remove the pan from the heat and keep warm.

9   Place the fish, skin-side down, in the ovenproof pan, turn the heat to medium-low, cook for about 3 minutes. Transfer the pan to the oven and cook for another 3 to 4 minutes.

10 Divide the mustard greens, beets, bacon, and radishes among three bowls. Top each with the fish and then pour the sauce over the fish. Garnish with the horseradish and mint leaves. Serve immediately.

6 VINEGAR-BASED DESSERTS

To be honest with you, I'm not a pastry chef. I didn't train to make world-renowned croquembouche or laminated doughs. But as a chef, I find myself more often than not in a place where I'll have to whip up some sort of dessert to build a menu, to please my in-laws, or to win a competition under intense pressure on *Chopped*. The following confections all flaunt the sweet-and-sour whimsicality that I love in a dessert based on vinegar.

Of course, most people wouldn't consider vinegar to be the foundation for any sweet treat. Hell, ask anyone who's not familiar with kitchen life about vinegar-based desserts and you'll probably get a blank stare, as you see them conjuring images of malt vinegar dousing a perfectly good soufflé. But when you stop to think about vinegar and dessert colliding, the combination makes perfect sense. Consider how many sweets contain citrus; therefore, swapping for vinegar—a fine acidic substitute—is like the Cavs taking out J. R. Smith for Kyle Korver. They're both going to work for the end product.

It's also worth noting that lemon is lemon—meaning, it can only do what lemons do. Vinegar comes in all sorts of flavors, tastes, colors, and aromas. Think of vinegar's potency on desserts as you would a good mixtape; if your whole tape is heavy metal, it'll be one-note and suck. But if you kick off with some metal, then ease into some thrash, and then follow that up with some soul, things get interesting. Vinegar's complexity does the same damn thing for your dessert.

This chapter reflects the treats that I've picked up along the way—the sources of which include chef friends, long-ago sabbaticals to Rome, and spontaneous fishing trips I took to the Florida Keys when I interned in Miami.

MOLDY MUSKMELON
(OR SUPER-RIPE PEACHES OR, WELL, ANYTHING THAT'S SUPER-RIPE)

Serves 6

3 tablespoons
unsalted butter

1 tablespoon "gold
standard" olive oil
(see page 23)

1 teaspoon kosher salt

1 medium ripe-as-hell
muskmelon, Charentais
melon, or cantaloupe,
peeled and sliced
1-inch thick

2 tablespoons raw
dark honey (preferably
chestnut or buckwheat)

1 tablespoon Old-School
Red Wine Vinegar
(page 34), sherry vinegar
(see variation, page 34),
or balsamic vinegar

1 cup House-Made
Ricotta (see page 206)

1 tablespoon pine nuts,
toasted and halved

Not many cultures celebrate the lowly muskmelon quite as the French, Italian, and Japanese do. They get it. I do, too, and I love it. One fall, a few years back, I decided to push the limits of melon ripeness and used the muskmelon as my specimen. I asked Floyd, a dreamy, blue-eyed farmer friend from Red Basket Farm in Kinsman, Ohio, for a case of ripe melons. I stored the melons at room temperature on perforated racks until the entirety of the bumpy, pale-skinned exterior turned moldy. When this happened, I knew that every last starch inside the melon had converted to a funky ferment. After carefully peeling the moldy exterior away, the golden, sexy flesh proved to be truly royal. I then warmed the flesh in a pan with brown butter and served it with Ohio buckwheat honey, pine nuts, aged red wine vinegar, and freshly made cheese. Voilà, it was the single most interesting bite of dessert I've ever created. For your own purposes, feel free not to age your melon; however, understand that ripeness is paramount, and some things are worth the wait. Peaches, prune plums, or any fruit that is ripe and local to your region will work just as well.

1 In a large stainless-steel sauté pan over medium-high heat, combine the butter, olive oil, and salt and cook, stirring occasionally, until the milk solids start to brown, about 3 minutes. (When it's just right, it'll smell like caramel popcorn.) Add the melon and, using a spoon, gently baste it with the butter for 1 minute. The fruit should be so ripe that you can't flip it for fear of breaking the flesh. Remove the pan from the heat and then add the honey and vinegar, swirling the pan to loosely combine. Set aside.

2 Smear the ricotta cheese on serving plates or a platter, creating a landing strip for the sweet-and-sour melon sauté. Place the warm melon on the cheese, pour the pan sauce over each melon slice and onto the cheese, and garnish with the pine nuts. Serve immediately.

JELLED VINEGAR

Makes about 1 quart; serves 6 to 8

½ cup raw apple cider

1½ tablespoon unflavored powdered gelatin

1 cup big, unabashedly Californian red wine (like a Cabernet)

1 pint frozen cranberries

¼ cup sugar

1 tablespoon peeled and grated fresh ginger

1 tablespoon Old-School Red Wine Vinegar (page 34)

This recipe is simple—childish even—but that's what makes it so fun. It's a great garnish for foie gras *au torchon*, chicken liver mousse, a cheese plate, Thanksgiving turkey, or even part of your petits fours thank-you plate for party guests. Whip it out whenever you see fit, really.

1   In a small bowl, stir together the apple cider and powdered gelatin and allow to bloom for 5 minutes.

2   In a blender, combine the wine, cranberries, sugar, ginger, and vinegar and puree until smooth. Transfer to a stainless-steel sauté pan over high heat and bring to a boil, stirring continuously to dissolve the sugar and cook the cranberries, about 4 minutes. Turn the heat to medium-high and simmer for 4 minutes to cook off the alcohol, then remove from the heat. Add the gelatin-cider mixture, whisk to combine, and let cool to room temperature.

3   Pour the mixture into a 8 by 3-inch terrine mold or a 12-inch baking dish and refrigerate until it's set, about 2 hours. Cut into desired shapes, cubes, or circles; using a cookie cutter if you wish. The jell will keep in an airtight container, refrigerated, for up to 7 days.

MULLED PORT & CHERRY GRANITA

Serves 6 to 8

½ cup Ruby Porto

½ cup sugar

1 pound fresh cherries, pitted, or a dark fruit like blackberries, blueberries, or pomegranate

3 whole star anise

3 allspice berries

8 black peppercorns

4 green cardamom pods

1 tablespoon peeled and sliced fresh ginger

½ cup water

¼ cup balsamic vinegar

I have a problem with Popsicles. Late at night, when the kids, dogs, and my wife are asleep, I wander outside and consume anywhere from five to fifty Popsicles while catching up on some Vonnegut or events in the newspaper, or watching HBO. This recipe was born out of my frugal restaurant-owner brain and, more important, my bona fide Popsicle addiction.

1 In a blender, combine the Porto, sugar, and cherries and puree on high speed until smooth. Tie the star anise, allspice, peppercorns, cardamom, and ginger in a piece of cheesecloth to make a sachet.

2 In a medium stainless-steel saucepan over medium heat, combine the water, cherry puree, and spice pouch and, stirring, bring to a boil. Then, turn the heat to low and simmer for 10 minutes to fully dissolve the sugar and incorporate the spice flavors. Remove from the heat, stir in the vinegar, remove the spice sachet, and let cool to room temperature.

3 Pour the mixture into a shallow baking dish and put in the freezer. Using a fork, stir and scrape it every 20 minutes until it's crystalline and frozen, 2 to 4 hours.

4 Serve immediately in coupe glasses with small spoons.

ICE ICE BABY

Here's the cool (and perhaps frustrating) part about granita. You have buku options for freezing; it is up to you and your level of commitment. Texturally, the difference between the beginner and badass versions is the crunchiness. Your beginner's version will result in a delicious Popsicle-like texture, while the badass iteration will produce a silky smooth scoopable Parisian sorbet. Here are the methods to try.

BEGINNER Seal the mixture in a quart ziplock bag and then place that bag into a gallon bag of ice and salt. Shake until frozen, about 30 minutes.

INTERMEDIATE Check out an old infomercial phenom that actually works wonderfully, the Play and Freeze.

EXPERT Pour the mixture into an ice-cream maker and follow the manufacturer's instructions for a delicious sorbet texture.

BADASS Go Pennsylvania Dutch—or Oaxaca village–style with a hand-cranked or hand-stirred ice-cream maker of ice and rock salt.

BOMB-ASS BOMBOLONI

Makes about 20 bomboloni

½ cup lukewarm (105°F) water

Two ¼-ounce envelopes active dry yeast

2 tablespoons honey

3 cups all-purpose flour

1 tablespoon granulated sugar

6 egg yolks

4 tablespoons whole milk

3 tablespoons salted butter, at room temperature

2 teaspoons kosher salt

¼ cup confectioners' sugar

1 cup Raspberry-Vinegar Jam (page 192)

3 cups canola oil

Just like everyone else in America, I eat my fair share of doughnuts while working at my desk. They're one of the rare foods that I'll never turn down. This recipe produces doughnuts that are so incredible and so very easy to make that I keep a miniature fryer in my office so I can quell any late-night cravings I might have.

1   In a small bowl, combine the water, yeast, and honey and stir to mix. Leave at room temperature until active and foamy, 10 to 20 minutes.

2   In the bowl of a stand mixer fitted with the hook attachment, combine the flour and granulated sugar and mix at medium-low speed for 15 seconds. Add the egg yolks, one at a time, and mix until combined, about 1 minute.

3   With the mixer at medium-low speed, drizzle in the water-yeast-honey mixture, then the milk. Add the butter and mix until the batter is smooth and has no lumps, 2 to 5 minutes. Finally, add the salt and mix for 30 seconds to combine. Cover and refrigerate the mixture for at least 1 hour or, preferably, up to overnight.

4   Evenly divide the confectioners' sugar among four brown paper bags and fill a small disposable pastry bag (with pastry tip) or a sandwich bag with the jam. Set aside.

5   On a lightly oiled work surface, position the dough and then cover with an oiled piece of parchment paper. Roll the tacky dough into a ½-inch-thick sheet. Discard the parchment and use a ring mold or biscuit cutter to cut out about twenty 1½-inch rounds.

6   In a large saucepan over medium-high heat, warm the canola oil to 350°F on an instant-read thermometer. Add three to six rounds at a time and fry, using a slotted spoon to flip them when they are golden brown and puffy, about 4 minutes. Continue to cook for a few minutes more to evenly brown them. Remove the bomboloni from the oil with the spoon and drain them on a resting rack or paper towels.

7   While the bomboloni are still warm, poke the pastry tip into each and stuff with about 1 tablespoon jam; if you're using a plastic bag, slice off a corner and squeeze the jam into the bomboloni. As soon as they're stuffed, toss four or five at a time into each brown paper bag, then shake them vigorously to coat with confectioners' sugar. Serve immediately.

CONTINUED

RASPBERRY-VINEGAR JAM *Makes about 1 quart*

4 cups fresh or frozen
raspberries

4 cups sugar

¼ cup Old-School Red
Wine Vinegar (page 34)

¼ cup water

Put the raspberries in a high-sided saucepan and mash them with your hands until they are broken up into chunky pieces. Add the sugar, vinegar, and water and bring to a boil over high heat. Boil until the mixture doubles in volume, about 2 minutes. Then, remove it from the heat and pour into a heatproof container, like a metal bowl. Allow the jam to cool to room temperature. Store in an airtight container, refrigerated, for up to 3 months.

PEACH PANNEKOEKEN

Serves 4

2 large, ripe peaches, sliced

3 cups water

3 eggs

2 tablespoons white wine vinegar (see variation, page 34)

1 teaspoon kosher salt

3 cups all-purpose flour

½ teaspoon baking soda

½ cup salted butter, melted

This is a South African pancake/crepe hybrid that has its roots in Dutch colonialism. What I like about it is that it can easily replace crepes in a dessert or savory dish, and it can definitely fill in for pancakes at breakfast. One food with multiple uses? Now that's something you should always get down with.

1 In a blender, combine half of the peaches, the water, eggs, vinegar, and salt and blend on high speed. Add the flour and then the baking soda, continuing to blend. With the blender still running, drizzle in ¼ cup of the melted butter and blend until smooth. Allow the batter to rest for at least 30 minutes—but no more than 3 hours—at room temperature.

2 Preheat the oven to 350°F.

3 In a medium nonstick, ovenproof pan over medium-high heat, warm 1 tablespoon melted butter. Pour in ½ cup pancake batter and scatter one-fourth of the remaining peach slices on the batter. Cook until the pancake is golden on the bottom and small air bubbles peek through the top, 5 to 10 minutes. Flip the pancake and place the pan in the oven for about 5 minutes. Repeat until all of the batter is used; you can speed up the process by using multiple pans.

4 Serve as each pancake is finished, or keep warm in the oven to serve together.

NONNA'S COOKIES
(AKA BISCOTTI, OR GRANDMA'S DAY-DRINKING COOKIES)

Makes about 16 cookies

SWEET & SOUR CANDIED FENNEL

1 small fennel bulb, thinly sliced

¾ cup granulated sugar

½ cup champagne vinegar (see variation, page 34)

1 tablespoon Pernod, ouzo, or other anise-flavored liqueur

½ cup unsalted butter, at room temperature

1 cup granulated sugar

2 eggs, plus 1 egg white

1 tablespoon toasted and cracked fennel seeds

1 teaspoon pure vanilla extract

Zest of 1 lemon

2 cups all-purpose flour

1 teaspoon baking powder

1 teaspoon kosher salt

½ cup pine nuts

2 tablespoons raw sugar or Belgium rock sugar

These cookies, which are actually biscotti (meaning "twice-cooked"), are a delicious, fully dry, typically nut-based cookie. We call them Nonna's Cookies because Italian grandmas the world-over spend mornings cooking items for dinner as well as whipping up these delicious treats. The reason Nonna would cook them during the day is because they give her an excuse to pour a glass of vin santo in the middle of the afternoon to dip the cookies in "to make sure they are delicious."

So rather than watching the Cleveland Browns play and lose, pissing you off, use this recipe as your excuse to have an enjoyable Sunday Funday.

DISCLAIMER We promote responsible Sunday Fundays.

1 To make the candied fennel: In a small stainless-steel saucepan over high heat, combine the sliced fennel, granulated sugar, and vinegar and bring to a simmer. Add the liqueur, turn the heat to low, and continue to simmer, covered, for 20 minutes. Remove the pan from the heat and let cool. Using a slotted spoon, remove the fennel slices from the syrup, shaking off any excess syrup, and transfer to a resting rack. (The syrup is delicious drizzled over fruit or ice cream. Transfer to an airtight container and store in the refrigerator for up to 4 months.) Allow the fennel to dry in a 170°F oven for a few hours or in a dehydrator at 90°F overnight. There is very little moisture in biscotti, so the drier the fennel is, the better. It should have a texture and feel similar to dried fruit.

2 Preheat the oven to 300°F. Line a baking sheet with parchment paper. Lightly oil two 9 by 6-inch pieces of parchment paper.

3 In the bowl of a stand mixer fitted with the paddle attachment, cream the butter and granulated sugar at medium speed until light and fluffy, about 5 minutes. Then, turn the speed to medium-low and add the whole eggs, one at a time. Add the fennel seeds, vanilla, and lemon zest and mix until combined.

4 In a separate bowl, combine the flour, baking powder, and salt and sift them into running the mixer bowl.

CONTINUED

5   Once the dough is evenly mixed, add the candied fennel and pine nuts and mix for 30 seconds more to evenly distribute. This dough will be very sticky.

6   Divide the dough in half and place each half in the center of its own piece of oiled parchment paper. Use the parchment to help you roll the dough into two even 6-inch-long loaves, then transfer both to the prepared baking sheet. The loaves should be equidistant from each other and the edges of the sheet.

7   Whisk the egg white with a little water, brush on the loaves, and then dust the loaves with the raw sugar.

8   Bake until the loaves are light brown in color and cooked through, about 30 minutes. Remove the baking sheet from the oven (but leave the oven on) and let the loaves cool to the touch. Then, using a serrated knife, cut each loaf on the diagonal into 1-inch-thick slices. Place the slices back on the baking sheet, cut-side down, and bake for 10 minutes, then flip each biscotti and bake for an additional 10 minutes. Let them cool on the pan. Transfer to an airtight container and store, at room temperature, for up to 4 weeks.

APPLE TARTE TATIN

Makes one 10- to 12-inch pie

6 firm apples, such as Golden Russet, Arkansas Black, or Granny Smith, peeled and flat-quartered

1 teaspoon Apple Cider Vinegar (page 35)

6 tablespoons cold unsalted butter

½ cup sugar

2 tablespoons Cider Gastrique (page 198)

One 16-ounce package whole-butter puff pastry (French brands are great; King Arthur is also delish), cold (almost frozen)

Stabilized Whipped-Cream Topping (see page 204) or Roquefort cheese for serving (optional)

This is the apple pie that we Americans wish we had invented. It has an incredible ratio of crust to filling and completely enrobes itself in a luscious caramel. It's perfect, but I've updated it with a gastrique, a traditional sauce of vinegar and sugar. This recipe starts on the stove top and finishes in the oven. Select a baking pan that is thicker than a classic pie pan and can be used both on a stove-top burner and in the oven. A pan that evenly distributes the heat is paramount; an enamel one like Le Creuset or cast iron will work great.

1 In a medium bowl, toss the apples with the vinegar to prevent oxidation.

2 Cut the butter into thin pats and place in a 10- to 12-inch round baking pan, completely covering the bottom with a single layer. Sprinkle the sugar over the butter. Place the apple quarters in concentric circles in the pan, making sure the flat sides are down. Pack them tightly and in a single layer.

3 Place the pan over medium-high heat and cook until the butter and sugar have caramelized and all the moisture from the apples has evaporated, about 20 minutes. Remove the pan from the heat and let come to room temperature, then pour the gastrique over the top.

4 Cut the puff pastry to fit the pan and place it on top of the apple, caramel, and gastrique mixture. Crimp the edges of the dough to fit inside the pan and prick the pastry lid all over with a fork. (If you want, you can stop here and refrigerate the tarte for up to 1 day.)

5 Preheat the oven to 425°F.

6 Bake the tarte until the puff pastry has risen and turned golden brown, 10 to 15 minutes. Remove from the oven; let cool slightly, about 20 minutes; and then flip it, pastry-side down, onto a serving plate.

7 Slice the tarte into wedges and top with whipped cream, or serve with a hunk of Roquefort on the side, if desired.

CONTINUED

CIDER GASTRIQUE *Makes ½ to 1 cup*

½ cup sugar

¼ to 1 cup water

Kosher salt

¼ cup Apple Cider Vinegar (page 35)

¼ cup apple cider or apple juice

1 In a medium saucepan over medium-high heat, combine the sugar and ¼ cup of the water and cook, stirring constantly to avoid scorching, until the sugar melts and lightly caramelizes, about 10 minutes. Season with salt and add the vinegar, apple cider, and enough of the remaining ¾ cup water to deglaze the pan, scraping up any brown bits with a wooden spoon.

2 Bring the mixture to a boil, then turn the heat to low and allow the gastrique to simmer and reduce by three-fourths; it will be thick and syrupy, about 20 minutes. Keep a watchful eye as it cooks down because it will easily scorch and burn. Remove from the heat and let cool to room temperature. Transfer to an airtight, nonreactive container and store, at room temperature, indefinitely.

CHESS PIE

Makes one 10- to 12-inch pie

CRUST

1 cup ice water

2 teaspoons white wine vinegar (see variation, page 34)

3 cups all-purpose flour, or 2 cups all-purpose flour and 1 cup whole-grain flour

1½ teaspoons kosher salt

2 cups unsalted butter, frozen and then box-grated or small-diced

FILLING

¼ cup whole milk

2 tablespoons crème fraîche or best-quality sour cream

1 tablespoon white wine vinegar (see variation, page 34)

Seeds from 1 vanilla bean, halved lengthwise and scraped

4 eggs, at room temperature

1½ cups sugar

3 tablespoons semolina or cornmeal (if you're feeling Southern)

1 teaspoon kosher salt

½ cup unsalted butter, melted

The old saying "as American as apple pie" needs a revamp. While nobody's denying the Americanness of apple pie, another pie could also lay claim to our country's favorite dessert-based cliché: the custard delicacy known as chess pie. While there are many etymologies for the name of this pie, I find the following to be the most credible and interesting. The mother of our country, Martha Washington, published a recipe for "very good cheesecake without cheese curd" in the mid-eighteenth century. This recipe's name first was "cheese pie," but when it eventually migrated to the Deep South, Geechee speakers changed it to "chess pie" over time. This pronunciation mirrors what they called sausage: "sauchess." Chess pie's long and interesting history stands as a testament to our country's historic attachment to the dessert—and the fact that we're not just about them apples.

I like to add a splash, or two, of vinegar in my pie crusts. It really helps cut some of the fattiness from the butter, which can sometimes be overpowering, and also helps to create a flakier crust. I also recommend cage-free organic eggs and grass-fed milk in the filling. You'll want to add them to all your pies once you taste the difference.

1 To make the crust: Preheat the oven to 350°F.

2 In a small measuring cup, combine the water and vinegar.

3 In a food processor, combine the flour and salt and pulse to mix. Evenly sprinkle the frozen butter over the flour and pulse until the dough combines and just begins to form small clumps. It will appear crumbly.

4 While pulsing the food processor, slowly drizzle in the water-vinegar mixture. The goal here is to work the dough and glutens only to combine the ingredients. So pulse minimally for a flaky crust. Once the dough is formed, remove from the food processor, flatten it into a puck, wrap in plastic, and refrigerate for at least 1 hour or up to 1 day.

5 On a lightly floured cutting board, unwrap the dough and, working quickly so you do not melt the butter and using a rolling pin, roll out the dough to a 15-inch-diameter circle that is about ¼ inch thick. There will be more than enough dough, so don't worry about rolling a perfect circle. Place the dough in a 10- or 12-inch pie pan, carefully press into the bottom, and crimp the edges. Place a parchment cartouche on top of the dough and add some old beans or pie weights to keep the crust from rising unevenly during the first bake.

6 Bake the crust for 10 minutes, then remove the weights and parchment and bake to get a golden brown color, about 4 minutes more. Remove from the oven and let the crust cool to room temperature.

7 To make the filling: Preheat the oven to 350°F.

8 In a small saucepan over medium-low heat, combine the milk, crème fraîche, vinegar, and vanilla seeds and bring to a simmer.

9 In a blender, combine the eggs, sugar, semolina, and salt (using a blender is not traditional, but it yields a silky smooth filling) and blend until thoroughly mixed, a couple of seconds. While the blender is still running, stream in the melted butter and then the warm milk-vanilla-vinegar mixture. Blend to fully combine the ingredients.

10 Pour the filling into the cool crust. Bake until the filling has mostly set, it should jiggle slightly in the center, about 40 minutes. (Store, covered and refrigerated, for up to 1 week.)

11 Slice the pie into wedges and serve warm or chilled.

NOTE To achieve maximum crust tenderness, think about biscuits and gnocchi as opposed to baguettes and pasta dough. The more your flour is stretched and worked, the toothier your dough will be. And for an extra-elegant (aka soigné) crust, before your second bake, brush the top with brown butter and sprinkle with coarse rock sugar.

KEY LIME-ISH PIE

Makes one 10- to 12-inch pie

GRAHAM CRACKER CRUST

1 cup graham cracker crumbs

¼ cups crumbled gingersnap cookies

1 teaspoon all-purpose flour

Pinch of kosher salt

2 tablespoons granulated sugar

5 tablespoons unsalted butter, melted

FILLING

4 egg yolks, at room temperature

1¾ cups sweetened condensed milk

½ cup rice vinegar (see variation, page 34)

Zest and juice of 1 Key lime

STABILIZED WHIPPED-CREAM TOPPING

2 tablespoons water

1 teaspoon unflavored powdered gelatin

1 cup cold heavy whipping cream (for optimal results, make sure the butterfat content is 4% or more)

2 tablespoons confectioners' sugar

From Hemingway to the debauchery of Fantasy Fest to my engagement on the country's southernmost beach, the Florida Keys hold a special place in my heart. This recipe is meant to sub vinegar in for some—if not all—of the Key lime in the traditional pie. I'm confident that Keys natives will appreciate this twist on their famed dessert, even if we're doing away with some of their beloved fruit (you can do the citrus-for-vinegar swap easily on a lemon curd or lemon meringue pie, too).

Homemade whipped cream tastes more regal and luxurious if you add gelatin, which will help it stay airy for days in the refrigerator. You should eat this pie cold—it helps to balance the sweetened condensed milk's sugar and the acid—while sipping a proper rum daiquiri and reading *Death in the Afternoon* or *The Sun Also Rises*. All will be bliss.

1 To make the graham cracker crust: Preheat the oven to 350°F.

2 In the bowl of a stand mixer, combine the graham cracker crumbs, gingersnaps, flour, salt, and granulated sugar. With the mixer at low speed, drizzle in the melted butter to bind the ingredients. Spread the mixture in a 10- to 12-inch pie pan, pushing and packing it with your hands into a tight ¼- to ⅓-inch-thick layer.

3 Bake until the crust is golden brown, about 10 minutes. Bake any remaining crumbs alongside on a baking sheet for a crunchy garnish, if desired. Remove from the oven and let cool to room temperature. (The crust will keep, covered and refrigerated, for up to 2 days.)

4 To make the filling: In the bowl of a stand mixer fitted with the whisk attachment, whip the egg yolks at medium-high speed for 2 minutes to add some air. Drizzle in the sweetened condensed milk and continue to whisk until light, airy, and fluffy, about 5 minutes. Stop the mixer, scrape down the sides of the bowl, and then sprinkle in the vinegar, lime zest (reserve some for garnish), and lime juice. Gently fold the filling a few times to incorporate the ingredients.

5 Pour the filling into the cooled crust. Bake until the filling is almost set, it should jiggle slightly in the center, about 30 minutes. Remove from the oven and let cool to room temperature, then refrigerate for up to 1 week.

6 To make the topping: Place a mixer bowl and whisk attachment in the freezer to chill for 30 minutes.

7 In a small, microwave-safe glass bowl, stir together the water and gelatin, then let sit and bloom for 5 minutes. Stir again and microwave on high for 15 to 30 seconds. Stir again and allow it to cool to room temperature.

8 Put the chilled bowl in the stand mixer and attach the whisk. Add the heavy whipping cream and whip at low speed while slowly streaming in the confectioners' sugar until stiff peaks form; the cream should stand on the whisk when lifted from the bowl. Once the sugar and cream are combined, add the room-temperature gelatin-water mix, turn the speed to medium-high, and whip to soft peaks, about 5 minutes. Scrape down the sides of the bowl periodically while whipping.

9 Slice the pie into wedges and serve garnished with whipped cream, some reserved lime zest, and toasted crumbs, if desired.

SENIOR'S RICOTTA CHEESECAKE

Makes one 10- to 12-inch cheesecake

HOUSE-MADE RICOTTA

2 quarts whole milk

2 cups heavy whipping cream

3 tablespoons white wine vinegar (see variation, page 34)

½ teaspoon kosher salt

⅔ cup sugar

¼ cup all-purpose flour

2 eggs, plus 6 egg yolks, at room temperature

1 teaspoon white wine vinegar (see variation, page 34)

½ teaspoon pure vanilla extract

½ teaspoon kosher salt

¼ teaspoon grated nutmeg

Zest and juice of 1 lemon

Graham Cracker Crust (see page 204), baked in a 10- or 12-inch springform pan

Macerated fresh fruit for serving

When I was working for Michael Symon as the chef de cuisine at Parea in NYC, I lived just off Flatbush Avenue in Brooklyn. There were many nights that I would get off the train and pop into Junior's on my way home for a quick late-night bite. After a while, this became a ritual for me, and I literally got to the point that I couldn't fall asleep at night without first eating a piece of their famous cheesecake.

Making the cheese for this recipe is super-easy. In my first *Iron Chef* battle, we were able to adapt and execute this recipe in the sixty-minute time constraint, season it, and then use it to fill ravioli. Once you make this, you'll never purchase ricotta again. Take it from me, it's simply cheaper to make your own tasty version. (And this recipe yields about 2 pounds.) After you make the ricotta, save the whey, the liquid left over after the curds have been separated out of the cheese, for baking, marinades, brines, kefir, and many other uses.

My love affair with cheesecake continues to this day. Here's my iteration of Junior's dessert; you will need a 10- or 12-inch springform pan.

1 To make the ricotta: In a large stainless-steel saucepan over high heat, combine the milk and cream and bring to simmer, 5 to 10 minutes. Use an instant-read thermometer to ensure that the temperature stays at or near 190°F. Then, turn the heat to low, add the vinegar and salt, and let simmer, stirring continuously and gently, until the milk curdles, 3 to 5 minutes. Remove from the heat and let the curds and whey sit and separate.

2 Line a strainer with cheesecloth and set over a bowl.

3 After at least 30 minutes, and no longer than 60 minutes, pour the mixture into the prepared strainer and let strain, uncovered, in the refrigerator for 24 hours. (Strained ricotta will keep in an airtight, non-reactive container, refrigerated, for up to 2 weeks. The whey will keep in an airtight, nonreactive container, refrigerated, for up to 3 months.)

4 Preheat the oven to 300°F.

5   In the bowl of a stand mixer fitted with paddle attachment, beat together the sugar, flour, eggs, and egg yolks on medium-low speed until combined. Add the vinegar, vanilla, salt, nutmeg, lemon zest, and lemon juice and continue to beat to incorporate. Then, add the ricotta and beat until evenly combined.

6   Pour the batter into the cooled crust. Wrap the outside of the springform pan with aluminum foil and place in a large roasting pan. Place the roasting pan (with the springform pan in it) on the oven rack and pour warm water into the roasting pan until it reaches three-fourths of the way up the springform pan. The aluminum foil will keep the water from seeping into the pan. Carefully push the oven rack back into the oven.

7   Bake until the cheesecake slightly jiggles in the very center when it's gently shaken, about 45 minutes. (I like a soft-set cheesecake without any browning on top; therefore, "low and slow" is the way to go.) Remove the cheesecake from the water bath and let cool to room temperature; then cover and refrigerate for at least 1 hour or up to 1 week. Remove the sides of the pan.

8   Slice the cheesecake into wedges and serve garnished with macerated fruit.

BOCCANEGRA
(CHOCOLATE-VINEGAR CAKE)

Makes one 8- to 10-inch cake

2 cups sugar

¾ cup unsalted butter, at room temperature

1 egg, plus 1 egg yolk

2½ cups all-purpose flour

½ cup cocoa powder

1 teaspoon baking soda

½ teaspoon kosher salt

1½ cups stout or milk stout beer (preferably Mom Jeans from Hoof Hearted Brewing) or bourbon, if you're feeling randy

2 tablespoons Greenhouse Tavern–Style Craft-Beer Vinegar (page 32)

1 teaspoon pure vanilla extract

Ice cream, Stabilized Whipped-Cream Topping (see page 204), or Raspberry-Vinegar Jam (page 192) for serving

Every year, we host a "Metal as Fuck" dinner at the Greenhouse Tavern. As you can guess, everything we serve at the meal—from the burgers to the dessert—has a certain darkness to it, all of it inspired by the coolest evil crap we can think of. For example, take the backstory behind this vinegar-based cake. In the 1200s, an Italian dark-arts practitioner named Dracosia advised a powerful Genoan family during a war. When he failed to help them, he was prosecuted for practicing black magic and stripped of his name. The new name he and his descendants received was "Boccanegra," which means "black mouth."

Apologies for the following corniness, but when we first whipped up the dinner's chocolatey, boozy cake, I totally fell under its spell. And that's not even the best part about the cake; every single bite an attendee takes leaves his or her mouth pitch-black. I knew this cake was the perfect dessert for the "Metal as Fuck" dinner. It's a proper tribute to the (admittedly incompetent) darkness-loving weirdo. Now *that's* freakin' metal.

1   Preheat the oven to 350°F. Butter an 8- to 10-inch cake pan.

2   In the bowl of a stand mixer fitted with the paddle attachment, beat together the sugar, butter, egg, and egg yolk at medium speed until soft ribbons form, about 5 minutes. Turn the speed to low and slowly stream in the flour, cocoa powder, baking soda, and salt. Once combined, add the stout, vinegar, and vanilla and keep mixing to fully incorporate. Pour the batter into the prepared pan.

3   Bake until the cake is set, a toothpick inserted into the center comes out clean, 30 to 40 minutes. Let cool to the touch. (The cake will keep, covered and at room temperature, for up to 1 week.)

4   Slice the cake into wedges and serve topped with ice cream, whipped cream, or jam.

DOBOSH

Serves 8 to 10

CAKE

4 cups confectioners' sugar, plus more for dusting

8 eggs, separated, plus 3 egg yolks

½ teaspoon kosher salt

Seeds from 2 vanilla beans, split lengthwise and scraped

1 cup all-purpose flour

2 tablespoons whole milk

BUTTERCREAM

5 ounces bittersweet chocolate, chopped

3 egg yolks

¼ cup granulated sugar

Pinch of kosher salt

1 cup half-and-half

2 tablespoons unsweetened cocoa powder

2 tablespoons Greenhouse Tavern– Style Craft-Beer Vinegar (page 32) or good-quality balsamic vinegar

1¼ pounds unsalted butter, cut into tablespoons

Certain desserts are special to me as an Eastern European, strudel and kugel being two specific examples. But for my family, Dobosh is king. Because of my Hungarian lineage (my grandfather's last name was originally Szegedi), this dessert is in my DNA. Between the time it takes to make and the cost of the ingredients, it's a top-of-the-line cake. It was originally a dessert for the aristocracy, but because of our ability nowadays to procure these ingredients cheaply and easily, a whole new class of people can make it in their own homes.

To oversimplify, it's a chocolate crepe cake that's covered in burnt meringue. The process isn't an Easy-Bake recipe; get ready to spend your entire Saturday baking it. However, if you have parents or grandparents from the Old Country, one bite and they'll agree—it's the shit and worth the time to make. So in honor of Great-Grandma Szegedi, let's show you how to bake for a true Hungarian king or queen.

You'll need a blowtorch to brûlée the meringue that covers this cake.

1. To make the cake: Position two racks in the middle and lower-third of the oven and preheat to 350°F. Coat two 12 by 17-inch baking pans with cooking spray and line the bottoms with parchment paper; make sure to spray the parchment.

2. In the bowl of a stand mixer fitted with the whisk attachment, combine 2 cups of the confectioners' sugar, the egg whites, salt, and vanilla seeds and beat at medium-high speed until stiff and glossy, about 5 minutes. Scrape the mixture into a medium bowl and clean the mixer bowl.

3. In the clean bowl, combine the 11 egg yolks, flour, milk, and remaining 2 cups confectioners' sugar and beat at medium speed until smooth, about 3 minutes. Beat in one-fourth of the beaten egg whites to lighten the batter. Using a rubber spatula, fold in the remaining beaten whites until no streaks remain. Evenly divide and spread the batter in the prepared baking pans.

4. Bake until the cakes are golden and set, and a toothpick inserted into the center comes out clean, 12 to 15 minutes, shifting the pans from top to bottom and front to back halfway through baking. Transfer the finished cakes to resting racks to cool. (Once cool, you can wrap tightly in plastic and refrigerate for up to 3 days.)

2 tablespoons
Raspberry-Vinegar Jam
(page 192; optional)

MERINGUE

1 cup granulated sugar

½ cup water

3 egg whites

Pinch of kosher salt

5   To make the buttercream: Put the chopped chocolate in a medium bowl. In a second medium bowl, whisk together the egg yolks, granulated sugar, and salt until pale, about 2 minutes. In a medium saucepan, combine the half-and-half and cocoa powder and heat, whisking frequently, until it reaches 160°F on an instant-read thermometer.

6   Whisk the hot liquid into the egg yolks, then scrape the mixture back into the saucepan. Cook over medium heat, whisking constantly, until slightly thickened and the instant-read thermometer registers 160°F, about 4 minutes. Strain the mixture over the chocolate and let stand until the chocolate melts. Whisk the chocolate until smooth, add the vinegar, whisk again until smooth, and then let cool completely.

7   In the bowl of a stand mixer fitted with the whisk attachment, beat the butter until fluffy. Scrape the chocolate mixture into the butter and beat until smooth and creamy, 5 to 10 minutes.

8   Lightly dust the cooled cakes with confectioners' sugar and top each with a sheet of wax paper. Invert the cakes onto a work surface and carefully peel off the parchment. Cut each cake in half horizontally, yielding four 12 by 17-inch layers.

9   Spread some of the buttercream on all four cake layers; reserving plenty to frost the top and sides of the finished cake. If desired, drizzle the jam on the two layers that will be in the middle of the cake. Using palette knives, carefully lift and stack the cake layers on top of one another. Frost the entire cake with the remaining buttercream. Refrigerate the cake until well chilled, at least 2 hours but it's preferable to chill overnight.

10 To make the meringue: In a small saucepan, combine the granulated sugar and water and bring to a boil, an instant-read thermometer should read 240°F, washing down the side of the pan with a moistened pastry brush, as necessary.

11 Meanwhile, in a clean bowl of a stand mixer fitted with the whisk attachment, combine the egg whites and salt and beat at high speed until soft peaks form. Turn the speed to medium, slowly drizzle in the hot syrup, and beat until incorporated. Then, turn the speed to high and beat the meringue until stiff and glossy and the sides of the bowl are no longer warm, about 7 minutes.

12 Spread a thin layer of meringue all over the cake, then use the remaining meringue to form decorative swirls. Using a blow torch, brown the meringue all over. Refrigerate the cake for at least 1 hour or up to 3 days before serving.

7 DRINKS

To be frank, most people don't realize how integral a role vinegar plays in cocktails. It's just as important as bitters, lime juice, and fancy ice-cube shapes. And here, everyone has the opportunity to get boozy while setting their sinuses and their health right.

Furthermore, I love a great cocktail. There's something so romantic and seductive about a finely crafted mixed drink that is often missing from a pint of beer or glass of wine. The making of a cocktail requires the same amount of thought, skill, and intuition that is needed when composing a stunning plate of food. I'm continually left in a state of awe by the drinks that are born during crafting sessions that I have with my beverage team. I work hard to not only source local Ohio produce, meat, and seafood but also alcohol and other beverages. Watershed Distillery is a local Ohio distillery that my restaurants work closely with. If Watershed Distillery's liquor isn't available to you, find a local distillery you like and use their spirits.

Really, cocktails deserve their own chapter because of their versatility when it comes to incorporating vinegar. Not only can you spritz the following drinks with an assortment of vinegars, but doing so is insanely fun and connects the ideas that permeate the rest of the book. Now let's pour up with some sours.

BLOODY MARY SOUR

Makes 1 cocktail

Kosher salt or celery salt (optional)

2 ounces vodka

2 to 4 ounces Bloody Mary Sour Base (recipe follows), depending upon your lifestyle

Ice cubes

Celery stalk, pickle, green olive, or lemon slice for garnish (optional)

Vinegar, garlic, chile, anchovy, and tomato make a delicious pasta dish, but they're even better with vodka, patio season, and a hangover that needs curing. Hair of the dog is possibly the cause of and solution to all of your Sunday problems. Enjoy.

Salt the rim of a Collins or pint glass, if desired. Pour in the vodka, then fill the glass halfway with Bloody Mary base, stirring to blend. Add ice until the glass is full and then garnish with a celery stalk, pickle, green olive, or lemon slice, if desired. Serve immediately.

BLOODY MARY SOUR BASE   *Makes about 3 quarts*

1 quart water

One 28-ounce can whole peeled tomatoes

½ cup pickle mash (aka unsweetened pickle relish)

¼ cup Sriracha

2 tablespoons Old-School Red Wine Vinegar (page 34)

1 tablespoon Old Bay Seasoning

2 teaspoons ground cumin

2 teaspoons freshly ground pepper

1 teaspoon celery salt

1 teaspoon fish sauce

1 garlic clove, grated

In a blender, combine the water, tomatoes, pickle mash, Sriracha, vinegar, Old Bay, cumin, pepper, celery salt, fish sauce, and garlic and blend until smooth. Ideally, the base should be used when it's made; but, if necessary, transfer to an airtight, nonreactive container and refrigerate for up to 1 week.

BEETNIK VODKA TONIC

Makes 1 cocktail

1½ ounces Red-Beet-Infused Vodka (recipe follows), plus 3 reserved cooked beet cubes

1 teaspoon Old-School Red Wine Vinegar (page 34)

Ice cubes

2 ounces tonic water (preferably Fever-Tree Premium Indian brand)

1 sprig thyme

I'm not a vodka guy myself, but I love beats and beets so this vodka tonic is the ideal drink for me. This cocktail, between the vodka and tonic, is great for every season except for winter (it's just a tad too light for cold weather; I would go with brown, bitters, and stirred for my winter cocktails). We thank one of Greenhouse Tavern's OG bartenders, Dean Sauers, for bringing this cocktail to our attention; it's known lovingly around the restaurant as the Dean Sauers Sour. The beet-flavored vodka can be enjoyed in a Bloody Mary Sour (page 216), any other vodka cocktail, or whatever tickles your fancy.

In a Collins glass, combine the vodka, reserved cubed beets, and vinegar and muddle together. Fill the glass with ice, top with the tonic, and garnish with the thyme. Serve immediately.

RED-BEET-INFUSED VODKA *Makes about 3¼ cups*

1 large beet, peeled, top trimmed to 1 inch, tail intact, and cleaned well

One 750-ml bottle vodka (preferably from Watershed Distillery)

1 *To roast the beet:* Preheat the oven to 350°F. Wrap the beet in aluminum foil, place on a rimmed baking sheet, and roast until cooked through and tender when pierced with a paring knife, about 1 hour.

To boil the beet: Bring a pot of water to a boil over medium-high heat. Add the beet and boil until cooked through and tender when pierced with a paring knife, about 40 minutes.

2 Remove the beet from the heat and let cool completely. Cut the beet into small dice, reserving and refrigerating three cubes for each cocktail.

3 Place the remaining beets in an airtight, nonreactive 2-quart (or larger) container. Pour the vodka over the beets and allow to infuse in the refrigerator until the vodka is bright red, a couple days. Strain out and discard the beets. Store in the refrigerator, indefinitely.

ALL-OHIO VESPER

Makes 1 cocktail

2 ounces gin (preferably from Watershed Distillery)

½ ounce vodka (preferably from Watershed Distillery)

½ ounce Greenhouse Tavern–Style Craft-Beer Vinegar (page 32)

½ ounce simple syrup (see facing page)

Ice cubes

Strip of lemon peel

The Vesper is the cocktail made famous by one of the most iconic booze sippers of all time, James Bond. Author Ian Fleming placed the drink in his original Bond novel, *Casino Royale*, and it's named for the first Bond girl, Vesper Lynd. While you can't be James Bond, you can at least feel like 007 with Greenhouse Tavern's iteration. While most cocktail historians make fun of 007 for ordering his martinis "shaken not stirred," which essentially eliminates any herbal gin nuances and clouds your cocktail, I can appreciate a shaken cocktail if Bond cosigns it. However, be aware, this is a clinical-strength beverage, so sip gently.

1 In a cocktail shaker, combine the gin, vodka, vinegar, and simple syrup and fill with ice. Cover and shake vigorously for 2 minutes. Then, taste; if it's too strong, allow it to sit and let the ice cubes melt to balance out the ingredients.

2 Pour the cocktail into a coupe glass. Using the pointer finger and thumb on each hand, twist the lemon peel over the cocktail, releasing all of the essential oils and citrus aroma. Finally, rim the glass with the twisted peel and garnish. Serve immediately.

"SHAKE IT LIKE A POLAROID PICTURE" GIN FIZZ

Makes 1 cocktail

2 ounces dry gin (preferably Bombay Sapphire)

1 ounce heavy whipping cream

¾ ounce Greenhouse Tavern–Style Craft-Beer Vinegar (page 32)

½ ounce simple syrup (recipe follows)

1 egg white

4 dashes orange-blossom water

Ice cubes

2 ounces club soda

Orange zest for garnish

What separates the Greenhouse Tavern version of the gin fizz from all of the rest are two elements. First, we substitute vinegar for the citrus—farmhouse-ale vinegar specifically. This was former Greenhouse Tavern beverage director Terra Campbell's idea to introduce and imbue a bright, citrusy, and tart flavor. And second, we utilize a London dry gin to channel the classic version of the drink. It is also necessary to use heavy whipping cream for this cocktail as other types, including whole milk and soy milk, don't work. Is it a workout to make? Yes. Is it an emulsified cold vinaigrette? Kind of. Is it a beautiful, delicious cocktail? Hell yeah.

1 In a cocktail shaker, combine the gin, cream, vinegar, simple syrup, egg white, and orange-blossom water. Cover and shake vigorously until the ingredients are completely emulsified, 2 minutes. (Seriously, shake it like a Polaroid picture; it also helps to have a bar towel in order to improve your grip.)

2 Fill a Collins glass with ice to chill it. Top off the shaker with ice, and then vigorously shake the cocktail for 3 minutes more.

3 Discard the ice from the Collins glass. Strain the mixture into the chilled glass, top it off with club soda, and garnish with orange zest. Serve immediately.

SIMPLE SYRUP *Makes about 1½ cups*

1 cup sugar

¾ cup water

In a small stainless-steel saucepan, combine the sugar and water. Bring the mixture to a boil over high heat, stirring until the sugar is dissolved. Remove from the heat and let cool. Store in an airtight container, at room temperature, for up to 3 weeks.

ORANGE-VINEGAR SAZERAC

Makes 1 cocktail

Ice cubes

1 sugar cube

3 dashes Peychaud's bitters

1½ ounces rye whiskey

1¼ ounces Pernod

1¼ ounces white wine

1 barspoon Greenhouse Tavern–Style Craft-Beer Vinegar (page 32)

Strip of orange peel

Since 1850, French American New Orleanians have popularized two beloved yet distinct Sazeracs. The original Sazerac was a traditional style of brandy from France; currently, Sazerac is also a rye whiskey created by Buffalo Trace Distillery in Kentucky. However, "Sazerac" is most commonly associated with the cocktail we're preparing. French settlers found it easier to source American rye-style Sazerac than importing French Sazerac. Because of this sourcing ingenuity, we can now enjoy the seemingly simple yet complex drink (flavorwise) of vinegar, rye, and Pernod.

1 Fill a rocks glass all the way with ice. Let it chill while you prepare the other ingredients.

2 In a second rocks glass, muddle together the sugar cube and Peychaud's; it should look like there's been an accident in some sand once you're done. Add the rye.

3 Dump the ice from the chilled glass. Add the Pernod, wine, and vinegar and swish and rinse the mixture around the glass, then gently pour the liquid into the sink as you slowly turn the glass in a circular motion.

4 Strain the rye mixture into the chilled, rinsed glass. Using the pointer finger and thumb on each hand, twist the orange peel over cocktail, releasing all of the essential oils and citrus aroma. Finally, rim the glass with the twisted peel and garnish. Serve immediately.

BOURBON GINGER BABY

Makes 1 cocktail

1 tablespoon finely chopped cucumber, plus 2 cucumber slices

¾ ounce ginger simple syrup (recipe follows)

½ ounce white wine vinegar (see variation, page 34)

1 barspoon lemon juice

1 barspoon lime juice

1½ ounces bourbon (preferably from Watershed Distillery)

Ice cubes

In years past, our head bartender at Greenhouse Tavern, Jeff Rowe, made a variation of this cocktail that I couldn't get enough of, incorporating three surprising bedfellows: cucumber, vinegar, and bourbon. Like most chefs, I prefer my cocktails at the end of the night to be brown, bitter, and stirred in order to heal the day's wounds and prepare the mind for sleep. A bucket of bourbon cures whatever ails.

1 Place the chopped cucumber in a muddling glass, add the simple syrup and vinegar, and then muddle together; basically a nice smash-and-press technique, the mixture should be a bit pulpy because you want to release the cucumber essence to take away the sharpness of the vinegar. Add the lemon juice and lime juice, then the bourbon, and fill the glass with ice. Place a metal cocktail shaker on top of the muddling glass and shake, then let the concoction mellow for a minute and the ice to melt slightly.

2 Place more ice in a rocks glass and garnish the rim with the cucumber slices. Place a tea strainer inside a Hawthorne strainer, set it over your cocktail glass, and strain the contents from muddling glass into the rocks glass. Serve immediately.

GINGER SIMPLE SYRUP *Makes about 2 cups*

1 cup water

1 cup sugar

½ cup peeled and sliced fresh ginger

In a small stainless-steel saucepan over high heat, combine the water and sugar and bring to a boil, stirring until the sugar is dissolved. Add the ginger, turn the heat to medium-low, and simmer for 15 minutes. Then, remove from the heat and let cool to room temperature.

Strain out and discard the ginger. Store in an airtight container, at room temperature, for up to 3 weeks, or in the refrigerator for up to 3 months.

HONEY-APPLE SHRUB TODDY

Makes 1 cocktail

2 ounces Spiced Apple
Shrub (recipe follows)

1¼ ounces bourbon
(preferably from
Watershed Distillery)

1 cinnamon stick

1 lemon wheel

6 ounces hot water

"I wish I had the flu right now," said nobody ever. But whether you're suffering from a bug or not, this hot cocktail recipe will have you feeling warm and boozy—which are never bad states to be in (especially if you're under the weather). In the shrub, Greenhouse Tavern bartending wizard Brannen Morris uses honey and apples for sweetness and allspice berries and cinnamon for complexity, and the acidity of the cider vinegar rounds out this warm cocktail. The good news is you can make this drink without the booze, so enjoy, even if you have to drive home.

In a coffee mug, combine the shrub, bourbon, cinnamon stick, and lemon wheel. Top with the hot water and stir once. Serve immediately.

SPICED APPLE SHRUB *Makes about 1 quart*

1 pound tart apples,
like Honeycrisp, sliced

¼ cup sliced fennel

1 tablespoon
allspice berries

Zest of 1 lemon

1 cup pure honey

1 cup hot water

¾ cup Apple Cider
Vinegar (page 35)

3 cinnamon sticks

In an airtight, nonreactive container, muddle together the apples, fennel, allspice, and lemon zest. Add the honey, hot water, vinegar, and cinnamon sticks; seal the container; and shake for a couple of seconds to combine. Refrigerate for 3 to 4 days and then strain through a fine-mesh sieve or cheesecloth into another airtight, nonreactive container. Store in the refrigerator, indefinitely.

CIDER SPRITZ

Makes 1 cocktail

2 slices sweet baking apple, such as Winesap

1 teaspoon Apple Wine Vinegar (page 36)

1 ounce Calvados or apple brandy (preferably Tom's Foolery Applejack American Apple Brandy)

Dash of bitters

Ice cubes

4 ounces sparkling hard cider

Yes, I will drink a beer on ice. Yes, I will drink wine on ice. So yes, I will drink any spritz, a beverage that includes spritzer and a form of alcohol. The great thing about spritzes is you can use any booze to make them; white wine, red wine, Aperol. . . . In the case of the Aperol spritz, it's the preferred late-afternoon beverage of every Italian. From 4 p.m. to 7 p.m., they'll be downing it while munching on potato chips and smoking cigarettes. The formula is simple: equal parts booze and sparkling liquid, plus ice to increase its refreshing qualities and decrease the booziness. To make it more local and Cleveland-specific, I've introduced hard cider to honor the lauded apple growers in the region. Stir up this cocktail as the weather gets nicer and you move your drinking outside.

In the bottom of a Collins glass, muddle together the apples and vinegar. Add the brandy and bitters, stir, and then add ice to fill. Top with the sparkling hard cider. Serve immediately.

TERRA'S AUSTIN-TOWN TEQUILA-TINI

Makes 1 cocktail

Kosher salt

1½ ounces tequila (preferably Don Julio Añejo Tequila)

1 ounce white wine vinegar (see variation, page 34)

¾ ounce Cointreau or triple sec, depending on your lifestyle

¼ ounce olive juice, plus 1 olive

¼ ounce lime juice, plus 1 lime wedge

You know it's a party when margaritas and dirty martinis are involved. When former Greenhouse Tavern bar collaborator—and Austin, Texas, native—Terra Campbell made me a tequila-tini (also known as a Mexi-Mart) one day, I was skeptical. But her use of aged tequila, vinegar, and olive juice transformed the traditional margarita flavors into something next level. So skip the plane ticket and the South by Southwest festival crowd and enjoy this cocktail in your backyard.

1 Salt the rim of a coupe glass and set it aside. (Be careful that you don't have too much salt on the glass itself because there are other salty elements in the drink.)

2 In a cocktail shaker, combine the tequila, vinegar, Cointreau, olive juice, and lime juice. Cover and shake vigorously for 2 minutes. Pour the drink into the coupe, then skewer the olive and lime wedge and garnish. Serve immediately.

MEZCAL PALOMA

Makes 1 cocktail

Kosher salt

Ice cubes

2 ounces mezcal

½ ounce lime juice, plus
1 lime wheel (optional)

1 tablespoon rice
vinegar (see variation,
page 34)

4 ounces grapefruit-
flavored San Pellegrino

Grapefruit wedge for
garnish (optional)

Great NYC chef Jonathan Waxman once perfectly summed up the Paloma's greatness: "This has everything I want." It's true; the Paloma is refreshing, tart, and not very sweet. It eschews mixers for a handful of components (mezcal, lime, vinegar, and grapefruit San Pellegrino) that create the perfect drink.

If I'm ever at a public function or wedding with little to no good beverage options, I simply ask the bartender for a club soda with a splash of grapefruit and a double shot of mezcal (or tequila, if mezcal's not available). I then mix it myself as a Paloma. Cocktail hack accomplished.

1 Salt the rim of a rocks glass and then fill to the top with ice.

2 In a cocktail shaker, combine the mezcal, lime juice, vinegar, a pinch of salt, and 1 cup ice. Cover and shake briefly for 5 to 7 seconds.

3 Remove the shaker top and add the Pellegrino, then strain the liquid into the rocks glass. Garnish with the lime slice, if desired, or drop a grapefruit wedge into the cocktail, or both. Serve immediately.

GLOSSARY

ACETOBACTER(IA) The main bacteria associated with open-air acid creation (aka making vinegar). These bacteria "eat" alcohol and "poop" acetic acid. The acetic acid produced by these bacteria is what gives vinegar its tangy bite. *Acetobacter* is also the genus of this bacteria.

AIR A mix of hydrogen, nitrogen, oxygen, and other gasses, what we breath. *Acetobacter* need oxygen in the air to live and produce vinegar.

ALCOHOL A building block in the vinegar-making process that is created through fermentation. You can obtain alcohol by purchasing it or you can make it (see page 42).

ANIMAL FATS Fats of animal origin used for cooking. These fats are melted down, or *rendered,* in which the impurities are removed. *See* Rendered Fats, Schmaltz, Suet.

BACTERIA These are the microscopic life forms needed to create fermented foods such as vinegar.

BAIN-MARIE A container holding hot water into which a pan is placed for slow cooking.

BEER A fermented alcoholic beverage based on grains, aka a gift from the gods.

BRAISING A wet cooking method that involves submerging a partial or whole ingredient in a liquid and then cooking it over low heat for a long time.

BRINE A mixture of water, salt, and/or sugar that is used to cure or pickle foods. A wide variety of spices and flavorings can be added. Brined foods are juicier and more flavorful.

BRODO Italian for "broth" or "stock," this is a vegetable stock that uses pasta, rice, or another starch to give it body and a richer mouthfeel in order to mimic a bone-based broth.

BUTTERCREAM A version of pastry cream without eggs. Often used as a frosting.

BUTTERFAT Also know as *milk fat*, these are the particles separated out from dairy when producing cream and butter. Here are the percentages of butterfat that top-line dairy products contain: milk is less than 3 percent butterfat; cream is 36 percent and higher, although great heavy whipping creams are 43 percent and up; cheese, or anything that's not cottage cheese, is 40 to 60 percent; and butter is 80 percent and above.

CARBON DIOXIDE (CO_2) As it pertains to the book, when carbon dioxide is created anaerobically, it equals carbonation, like champagne bubbles. It is also the by-product produced as bacteria and yeasts ferment foods and liquids.

CELLULOSE A complex carbohydrate that looks like a jellyfish and makes up the physical body that you see in a vinegar mother or a SCOBY.

CHEESECLOTH A type of cotton cloth used in cheese making and other culinary applications. Think of it as the original reusable coffee filter.

CORN/CORNED/CORNING These are very old terms relating to meat that has been cured with salt in a brine before cooking, such as corned beef. Traditionally large grains of salt, called *corns*, were specifically used for this technique.

CRUDO Literally translates as "raw" in Italian. We use this to describe any dish with raw protein, especially seafood.

CURE A technique in which salt and/or sugar is used to preserve food.

DEGLAZE To pour a liquid into a hot pan to help free flavorful bits of food stuck to the bottom.

DISTILLED VINEGAR Confusingly enough, distilled vinegar isn't distilled; it's a strongly acidic, extremely manipulated industrial version of white vinegar that's produced from a distilled alcohol such as vodka or moonshine.

DRIPPINGS The delicious and flavorful fats and juices that drip from a piece of meat when it cooks.

EMULSIFICATION A process of suspending two opposing liquids; suspension can be mechanically achieved or chemically induced. Mechanical methods include whipping egg yolks into butter to create hollandaise. Chemically induced methods can be achieved by adding an emulsifier, such as agar or lecithin, to butter, carrot juice, and vinegar to create a modern carrot beurre blanc. Examples of emulsified vinegar-based sauces include mayonnaise (egg, acid, oil), which is mechanically combined using a whisk or blender, and hollandaise, which is the same as mayo except it replaces oil with butter.

FINES HERBS A mixture of herbs that have soft stems, such as parsley, taragon, chives, and dill. These herbs have a much more delicate flavor than woody herbs, such as rosemary.

FOND French for "background," fond commonly refers to the browned bits and caramelized drippings of meat and vegetables that are stuck to the bottom of a pan after sautéing, searing, or roasting.

GARUM An ancient-Roman fish sauce that was used to provide umami.

GASTRIQUE A traditional sauce of vinegar and sugar; it's also known in Italy as *agrodolce*, literally "sour" (*agro*) and "sweet" (*dolce*).

GELATIN A collagen-based animal by-product that is used to congeal a cool liquid in everything from aspic to gelatin to pharmaceutical medicines to shampoo. Many available vegetarian substitutes, like agar, are derived from algae and seaweed. It's available in powdered form (which we use for recipes in the book) and sheets (which we use at the restaurant). Like iocane powder, it's scentless, tasteless, and odorless.

GERMS A cheeky term we use in place of SCOBY or mother, with both positive and negative connotations, including but not exclusive to organisms, bacteria, and yeasts.

HONEY Honey is now readily available in many different varieties, like dark (chestnut or buckwheat) and light (orange blossom or wildflower) based on the diet of the bee that produces it. Typically, the darker the honey, the more robust and bitter the flavor; the lighter the honey color, the less intense its flavor.

JAM/JELLY Jam is a condiment based on combining sugars, fruit, fruit juices, and pectin. Jelly is a filtered-fruit-juice-based condiment that combines sugar, pectin, and, well, fruit juice.

JUICE The liquid you're trying to turn into a vinegar before alcohol is created or added. The flavor of the juice is eventually what the flavor will be in the vinegar; for example, using carrot juice, apple juice, hard cider, beer, or wine.

LONDON BROIL Traditionally, this was a way to cook beef, not an actual cut of meat. In recent years, unscrupulous butchers have given this name to various cuts from the top round of beef that comes from the back leg(s).

MARINATING A technique in which a food is submerged and soaked in a highly seasoned and flavorful liquid. This can be done before or after cooking, depending on the food and the desired results.

MERINGUE A dessert or garnish that is based on egg whites and sugar and has been whipped to incorporate air; it's also the basis for marshmallows, Pavlova, baked Alaska, and many other desserts.

MISO A very ancient food with origins in China but most often associated with Japan. It is made by mixing cooked soybeans, barley, salt, and a mold called koji together and letting it age and mature for many months or years. It is a delicious savory and salty condiment.

MOTHER A colony of *Acetobacter*. Can also mean any starter culture used in various ferments.

OXIDIZATION A chemical process in which oxygen binds or reacts with other elements and molecules. When foods oxidize, they turn brown; a cut apple is a good example.

PAN SAUCE A sauce built in a pan using the fond from a food that was just cooked in the pan.

PÂTE À CHOUX/PATE CHOUX A light and airy pastry dough made from flour, butter, water, and eggs. It serves as the dough used to make eclairs, churros, crullers, and quenelles.

pH SCALE A measure of acids and bases on a scale from 0 to 14. Most vinegars—acids—have a pH of 3 to 4.5 on this scale. Neutral items, like water, have a pH of around 7, and lye, a base, has a pH of 13.

POACHING A wet method of preparation in which a liquid, usually water or a water-based liquid but sometimes oil, is held at approximately 160°F and foods are submerged in it to gently cook.

POT ROAST Like London broil (see entry), this is a way of cooking meat, typically beef, not an actual cut. Common cuts of beef used for pot roast include those from the chuck, brisket, and round; I use shin and shank.

QUENELLE A mixture meat or fish, cream, and pâte à choux formed into a football-shaped dumpling and then cooked, usually by poaching.

RENDERED FATS Animal fats cooked in a manner that melts the fat and removes the impurities that can easily burn during cooking.

RESTING RACK A wire rack used to rest food on. It can fit inside a roasting pan to keep an item from contact with the fat and juices that run off it during cooking. It allows even heat to surround the food while it cooks.

ROASTING PAN A large rectangular pan with fairly deep sides that is used to roast larger cuts of meats or whole animals.

ROOM TEMPERATURE A rule for all proteins: Don't be afraid of room temperature, which is considered to be 68° to 78°F. Fish, tofu, pork—whatever it is—cooks more evenly from room temperature. So season that meat and leave it out at room temperature for a couple of hours or even up to a day.

SACHET A small cheesecloth sack filled with herbs and spices.

SCHMALTZ Rendered poultry fat, specifically chicken, although duck, turkey, goose, and other fowl can also be used to make schmaltz.

SCOBY An acronym for Symbiotic Colony of Bacteria and Yeasts, which is used to produce kombucha, vinegar, and other fermented goods.

SEAM A way of butchering meat that separates individual muscles from each other. The place where two muscles meet is also a *seam*.

SEAR To cook something in a very hot pan so as to caramelize and brown the surface.

SHIN A portion of meat from the lower part of an animal's leg cut from right above the trotter (foot).

SUET The hard fat found around the kidneys and other organs in beef. It has a very high smoke point and is great for frying.

TIME Unit of measurement used when creating vinegar. The best way to commit the idea of time in the process of making vinegar is to remember what Gollum said to Bilbo Baggins in *The Hobbit*: "This thing all things devours; birds, beasts, trees, flowers; gnaws iron, bites steel; grinds hard stones to meal; slays king, ruins town; and beats high mountain down." Simply put, time is a necessary ingredient in making vinegar.

VINEGAR An acetic acid that is secreted by an *Acetobacter* when it consumes alcohol. Chemically speaking, vinegar's pH should be between 3 and 4.5 on the pH scale. Vinegar is different from pure acetic acid in that it contains various flavors, tastes, and aroma molecules that make it delicious. You wouldn't want to touch or consume pure acetic acid.

WILD MUSHROOMS Mushrooms that are foraged from areas not under cultivation. If you see this term on a package of oyster and shiitake mushrooms at your local grocer, your grocer is lying to you. Truly wild mushrooms aren't cultivated, are somewhat rare, and tend to be extremely tasty and expensive.

WINE A fermented alcoholic beverage made from fruits or vegetables. Grapes are used most often.

YEAST A single-cell microorganism that eats sugar and produces alcohol and carbon dioxide. It's a part of SCOBY or mother, and it can be found naturally present everywhere from apple skins to the air we breathe. It requires moisture and exposure to oxygen in order to activate. There are two main types used in baking. Dry active yeast is a shelf-stable, powdered version; cake yeast is a refrigerated live active product. There are many other yeasts available on the market, from brewer's to champagne, none of which we tackle in this book.

ACKNOWLEDGMENTS

FROM JONATHON

So I wrote a book, again.

NO

So we wrote a book, again.

True

As singular as the act of putting pencil to paper may appear, and even feel sometimes, when the first copy finally drops you realize you are standing on the shoulders of many hardworking friends, family, makers, directors, culinarians, photographers, artists, writers, researchers, historians, muses, and creators. As I am human and of an extremely forgetful nature, inevitably some people and stories may have been forgotten, unintentionally misrepresented, or inaccurately rendered. I got you, sorry I forgot, thank you for you and whatever you did, feel free to take to twitter (@chefsawyer) with any callouts you deem necessary. Much love.

In no particular order, thanks to:

AMELIA As William Shatner once said, "his muse." You are my best friend, lover, and wife. Our life is the fucking greatest. Thank you. Catcher and Louisiana, from your first bites of purloined food, I knew you would both be awesome. You guys are the meaning of life.

SHITTY VINEGAR PRODUCERS Your adjunct, colored, chemicaled, chapitalized, watery, sour juice provided the spark I needed to start this fire.

RYAN M. JOSEPH Your first interview with me was deliberate, thorough, super-long, and kind of annoying. The resulting article on the dining scene in CLE mirrored so precisely my sentiment. In the age of out-of-context quotes and fake media, accurate journalism needs to be championed.

COOKS From Daniel Boulud to "the new guy" and everyone in between, it has been my pleasure sharing the piano with you. Cooking with y'all is the reason, and no you can't have next Friday off.

KELLY, BETSY, AND OUR TEAM AT TEN SPEED Secretly known by the moniker "polite sharks," 'cause they are super-nice but will cut a bitch to get it done. Through your attention to detail and creativity, the personality of the book blossomed. While we were late on nearly every deadline, you always believed in us, trusted the voice, and pushed the process to completion. Mad Respect.

TO MUSIC For whatever cognitive neuro-scientific reason, I am able to do my finest deep work with a constant flow of tunes. Watch out for the "House Of Vinegar" compendium playlist of Lou Reed, Dolly Parton, Bright Eyes, Jonwayne, Angèle Dubeau, Frank Ocean, Emmylou Harris, Yo La Tengo, Ludovico Einaudi, the Ramones, Johannes Brahms, Kanye, and many more.

JEREMY UMANSKY My foraging, fermenting, fomenting friend, whose quest for gastronomic knowledge is unquenchable. When I first interviewed Jeremy for the position of Larder Master & Food Lab partner at Trentina, he brought a house-made yogurt and foraged BKLN blueberry parfait. I ate it. I hired him and the rest is history. The Best to you and yours, Jer. #vapelife.

THOSE INTREPID BABYLONIANS Your 5000 BC accidental discovery of vinegar forever changed food history.

THE PRE–ROMAN EMPIRE FRANCO-GERMANIC CELTS (MY ANCESTORS) You decided to transport goods in oak barrels for ease. Soon after, we realized that the vanillin oxidation and the other magic that happens inside an aging oak barrel makes everything taste better.

THE BROTHER I ALWAYS WANTED—MATT SWEENEY Brilliant artist, father, goofball, Little Tikes basketball champ, and Renaissance man.

PETE LARSON, CLAIRE VREDEVOOGD, AND CREW Knives, cameras, spoons, and motor-cycles; you created images that are singular and identifiable as *House of Vinegar*.

THE MATRIARCHS OF MY FAMILY WETZEL, SAWYER, AND SZEGEDI Your love of cooking, gardening, and gathering forever imprinted me with an appreciation for frugal, resourceful, and delicious food.

TO TEAM SAWYER I'm a pain in the ass, I know, and you all make it work, somehow, everyday.

THE DOGS, CHICKENS, AND GUINEA PIGS OF MY LIFE Bunny, Bear, Squid, Kilgore Trout, Acorn, Acorn Jr, Vito, Biscuit, Romeo, Potato, Clementine, Brenda Walsh, and all. Do you understand me when I'm talking to you? Doesn't matter really, you're always there when I need you. Love.

CLEVELAND AND NYC PUBLIC LIBRARIES Inspiration on tap. Get a library card, share books with your peers, collect books, and enjoy.

MY ACTUAL AND PROVERBIAL FAMILY My godmother, Aunt Steph, Sarah and Andy, Mom and Dad, Jeremiah and Michelle, Debi, AK, Becky Stacho, Katelyn, Jesse, Brian Goodman, and Vinnie V4.

FROM RYAN

First, thanks to Jonathon and Jeremy for allowing me to join this project. They're true mensches for letting me tag along on this journey. Second, thanks to my parents, Don and Michele, my grandparents, and friends for the love and support. And third, shout-out to everyone who put me onto this path in the first place: the whole First We Feast crew, including Chris Schonberger, Nick Schonberger, Justin Bolois, Sarah Honda, Jackson Connor, and Erin Mosbaugh; the guy who first gave me a career in writing, Ty "Gotty" King; my friend and editor, Khushbu Shah; and my friend and former boss who allowed me dip out of work to hang in Cleveland for days at a time, Erin Weaver.

FROM JEREMY

I would like to than my wife, Allie, and daughter, Emilia, for their undying support. A huge thanks also goes out to Jonathon Sawyer for having faith in me and being a great friend. Additional thanks go to Kenny Scott, Harry Rosenblum, Angel Zimmerman, Rich Shih, Sandor Katz, Ryan Joseph, and all my friends and family for their amazing support and willingness to be guinea pigs for my gastronomic endeavors.

UNACKNOWLEDGMENTS

None. Life is too short and precious to linger on misdeeds, shortcomings, and beefs. I choose to live in the day; all that past brought me here. I hold no ill will for any, and thank you for being a part of my story. Choose to be happy and positive. Surround yourself with good. The future of this ever-spinning rock—and beyond—is bright.

About the AUTHOR

HEY Y'ALL

From my first home-grown-tomato and onion sandwich to last night's roasted chicken with bread heels, I've journeyed to enjoy all the food and beverages of the world from the past, present, and future.

I was born in Chicago, raised in Cleveland, and lived and cooked in New York City, Pittsburgh, Miami, Rome, and Dayton for now.

Some people said I am good at food. James Beard Award, *Bon Appétit* best new restaurant list, *Esquire* best new restaurant list . . .

Some TV shows let me talk and compete with food—*Iron Chef America*, *Chopped Grill Masters*, *The Best Thing I Ever Ate*, *Cleveland Hustles*, *Bizarre Foods with Andrew Zimmern*, *Dinner: Impossible* . . .

The average human head weighs 13 pounds and the plural of *beef* is *beeves*.

I hire people almost automatically if they were wrestlers or are in the orchestra.

I'm addicted to podcasts, consuming more than 100 hours of information every week— Hardcore History, Keep It!, Last Podcast on the Left, 99% Invisible, Reveal, The Paris Review, and many more. Send me your recs!

Once, I sliced the top knuckle of my middle finger in the food processor while shredding a case of cabbage for kimchi. My chef Brian Goodman searched the cabbage, found the finger, and sent it to me in a pastry bag on ice at NYC's Lutheran Hospital. Carlos our garde manger cook delivered it; but when the doctor saw it, he laughed and threw it in the garbage. The finger works, but it never grew back.

Now, let me leave you with two gems and thank you for your time:

"The cause of, and solution to, all of life's problems."

—Homer J. Simpson
referring to alcohol, but applicable with food for me and many

"Find what you love and let it kill you. Let it drain from you your all. Let it cling onto your back and weigh you down into eventual nothingness. Let it kill you, and let it devour your remains. For all things will kill you, both slowly and fastly, but it's much better to be killed by a lover."

—Henry Charles Bukowski,
or maybe Kinky Freedman

INDEX

Steak Frites with Red Wine
    Vinegar Demi-Glace
    Beurre, 166–68
Strawberry Wine Vinegar, 42
sugar, 10
Sunday Gravy over Cavatelli,
    135–36
Symon, Michael, 95, 206

T

Tarte Tatin, Apple, 197–98
Tequila-tini, Terra's
    Austin-Town, 227
Tincture, Daily Vinegar, 45
Tofu Jerky, 147
tomatoes
    Bloody Mary Sour Base, 216
    Chickpea and Tomato
        LeBron (Not Steph) Curry,
        154–55
    Grilled Out-of-Season Tomato
        Sauce, 175
    House Ketchup, 78–79
    Noodlecat's Power Ketchup, 80
    Pickled Green Tomatoes, 52
    Ratatouille Nicoise, 162
    Sunday Gravy over Cavatelli,
        135–36
    Umami-Infused Vinegar, 44
    Walleye Pike Quenelles with
        Tomatoes, 175–76
turkey
    Holiday Yam Soup, Yemenite-
        Style, 153
turnips
    The Best Root-Vegetable
        Roast of Your Life, 137
    Whole Turnips Apicius with
        Garlic Garam Vinegar,
        Golden Raisins, Fennel
        Seed and Khlea, 156–57

U

Umami-Infused Vinegar, 44
Umansky, Jeremy, 40

V

vanilla schnapps
    Cream Soda Vinegar, 40
veal
    Sunday Gravy over Cavatelli,
        135–36
vegetables
    The Best Root-Vegetable
        Roast of Your Life, 137
    The Greenhouse Tavern
        Veggie Burger, 62
    Hot and Spicy Romanesco
        Giardiniera, 67
    See also individual vegetables
Vesper, All-Ohio, 220
vinaigrettes, 74–76
    Classic Maple Vinaigrette, 95
    Dijon Vinaigrette, 91
vinegar (general)
    fermentation and, 14
    power of, 5
    rating system for, 18
    terroir and, 19
vinegar making
    ABV and, 7–8
    equipment for, 13–14
    flies and, 9–10
    formula for, 19
    oxygen and, 8–9
    patience and, 10
    styles of, 7
    sugar and, 10
    thirteen commandments of,
        17–19
    with unusual ingredients, 11
vinegars (recipes)
    Apple Cider Vinegar, 35
    Apple Wine Vinegar, 36
    Begonia Vinegar, 41
    Cream Soda Vinegar, 40
    Garlic Garum Vinegar, 157
    Greenhouse Tavern–Style
        Craft-Beer Vinegar, 32
    Jelled Vinegar, 187
    Modernist Cucumber
        Vinegar, 39
    Old-School Red Wine
        Vinegar, 34

Prosciutto-Scotch Vinegar, 37
    Strawberry Wine Vinegar, 42
    Umami-Infused Vinegar, 44
vodka
    All-Ohio Vesper, 220
    Beetnik Vodka Tonic, 219
    Bloody Mary Sour, 216
    Red-Beet-Infused Vodka, 219

W

Walleye Pike Quenelles with
    Tomatoes, 175–76
Washington, Martha, 202
Watermelon Rind Pickle, 57
Waxman, Jonathan, 166, 229
Whipped-Cream Topping,
    Stabilized, 204–5
wine
    Apple Wine Vinegar, 36
    Begonia Vinegar, 41
    Dijon Mustard, 90
    Jelled Vinegar, 187
    Old-School Red Wine
        Vinegar, 34
    Orange-Vinegar Sazerac, 222
    Red Wine–Braised Lentils
        and Frisée Salad Dijon, 93
    Steak Frites with Red Wine
        Vinegar Demi-Glace
        Beurre, 166–68
    Strawberry Wine Vinegar, 42

X

XO à la Trentina, 112

Y

Yam Soup, Holiday, Yemenite-
    Style, 153

Published in the United States by Ten Speed Press, an imprint of the
Crown Publishing Group, a division of Penguin Random House LLC, New York.
www.crownpublishing.com
www.tenspeed.com

Ten Speed Press and the Ten Speed Press colophon are registered trademarks of
Penguin Random House LLC.

Library of Congress Cataloging-in-Publication Data
    Names: Sawyer, Jonathon, author. | Larson, Peter (Photographer)
    Title: House of vinegar : the power of sour, with recipes / Jonathon Sawyer ;
        photographs by Peter Larson.
    Description: First edition. | California : Ten Speed Press, 2018. | Includes
        bibliographical references and index.
    Identifiers: LCCN 2018010977 |
    Subjects: LCSH: Cooking (Vinegar) | Vinegar. | LCGFT: Cookbooks.
    Classification: LCC TX819.V5 S29 2018 | DDC 641.6/2—dc23
    LC record available at https://lccn.loc.gov/2018010977

Hardcover ISBN: 978-0-399-57916-5
eBook ISBN: 978-0-399-57917-2

Printed in China

Design by Betsy Stromberg
Food and prop styling by Claire Vredevoogd
Food styling assistance by Elly Vredevoogd

10 9 8 7 6 5 4 3 2 1

First Edition